Beyond Witnessing

Peter Chidi Okuma

Beyond Witnessing

A New Way of Humanising the World

PETER LANG
EDITION

Bibliographic Information published by the Deutsche Nationalbibliothek
The Deutsche Nationalbibliothek lists this publication in the Deutsche Nationalbibliografie; detailed bibliographic data is available in the internet at http://dnb.d-nb.de.

Library of Congress Cataloging-in-Publication Data

Okuma, Peter Chidi.
Beyond witnessing : a new way of humanising the world / Peter Chidi Okuma. — 1 [edition].
pages cm
Includes bibliographical references.
ISBN 978-3-631-64760-8
1. Church work with the poor—Catholic Church. 2. Poverty—Religious aspects—Catholic Church. 3. Prayer—Catholic Church. 4. Christian life—Catholic authors. 5. Religion and social problems. I. Title.
BX2347.8.P66O38 2013
261.8'325—dc23

2013024727

ISBN 978-3-631-64760-8 (Print)
E-ISBN 978-3-653-03529-2 E-Book)
DOI 10.3726/978-3-653-03529-2

Peter Lang Edition is an Imprint of Peter Lang GmbH.

Peter Lang – Frankfurt am Main · Bern · Bruxelles · New York · Oxford · Warszawa · Wien

www.peterlang.de

"We are called to live the love of God, not to feel the love of God. We live this love through prayer and action. Our work is the fruit of our prayer, so that if our work is not going well, we must examine our prayer life. If we neglect our work or are harsh, proud, moody, and angry, then we should examine our prayer life. We will see that something has gone wrong there."

- Mother Teresa of Calcutta, in ANGELO D. SCOLOZZI (ed.), MOTHER TERESA, Thirsting for God: A yearbook of prayers, Meditations, and Anecdotes, (St. Anthony Messenger Press), Cincinnati, 2000, p. 178.

Dedication

This book is especially dedicated in love to the Dötzer family – Pa Franz, Mum Maria, Elizabeth, Johannes, Ursula and Barbara

and

to my elder sister Chinyere

and
Rev. Sr. Evelyn Thompson

to all who have been truly there for me Most of All the Blessed Mother of God, Virgin Mary – the Queen of my Heart!

Table of contents

Preface

In my first book with Peter Lang Academic publishers, {New York, Brussels, Frankfurt am Main (2002)} titled: *'Toward an African theology: the Igbo context in Nigeria'*, under the academic series titled: *Gods, Humans and Religion*, edited by Gabriel Fragnière (Rector of the College of Europe Brussels, Belgium). I dealt with the term, *'appropriation'* – the appropriation of the gospel to concrete situations in the light of doing theology in a contextual situation of a people (Igbo of Nigeria), and its challenges as it finds a place in the Second Vatican Council in light of the *'aggiornamento' (renewal)* program of the Council.

In another book titled, *The Vatican II. The Laity and Today's Challenges (Peter Lang Academic Publishers, Frankfurt am Main, 2011)*, I took my argument from the first book on 'appropriation' of the gospel message in light of the Second Vatican Council to a new height. This height was the *"prophetic witnessing"* or what is often referred by some scholars as *'witnessing of life'*,[1] or *Testimonium* to deploy the 'deep-meaning-ful' word of the Katholieke Universiteit Leuven, Belgium Vatican II Historian Mathijs Lamberigts[2].

In the above work mentioned, I argued in light of the fact that all the baptized in Christ are called to this noble role in the Church and in the World as 'prophets' courtesy of their baptism. This line of argumentation finds it base in the Vatican II document that "the faithful who by Baptism are incorporated into Christ, are placed in the people of God, and in their own way share the priestly, prophetic and kingly office of Christ, and to the best of their ability carry on the mission of the whole Christian people in the Church and in the world" (*Lumen Gentium*, no.31).

As a fallout from today's developments in our world and the bastardization of this noble task of witnessing in concrete, it seems to this writer that a key issue has often been neglected in recent times in the light of (post) modern efforts of 'doing heroic works' of witnessing in the Church and in the (post) modern human society. This seemingly missing link is the linkage between good work and prayer – between 'charity and liturgy' – between '*vita contemplativa and*

1 Cf. JOEPH RATZINGER, POPE BENEDICT XVI, *Jesus of Nazareth – Holy Week: From the Entrance into the Jerusalem to the Resurrection,* San Francisco, pp. 50, 225.

2 This writer as a doctoral student researching on the laity and Vatican II Council at the KULeuven Belgium researched closely and personally with Professor Mathijs Lamberigts between 2001- 2005 when he was the Rector of the Faculty of Theology of Leuven Belgium. This Professor as a Dean then helped in supervising his doctoral research on the laity and Vatican II.

vita activa' so to say. My tone of argument is that they do no harm to each other but instead complement and interpenetrate each other, as was the case in the past epochs of the Church and the human society. A sole effort today to separate them and to live, and to live with this separation would not augur too well with the intricacy of humanizing our world today: active life needs contemplative life and vice-verse. Otherwise witnessing will be truncated into a mere *atheistic heroism*. And of course this would be an aberration of true *Testimonium (Witnessing)* as understood in the core message of Vatican II Council 50-year-on![3]

3 Cf. PETER HÜNERMANN U. BERND JOCHEN HILBERATH, (Editors & co.), *Herders Theologischer Kommentar zum Zweiten Vatikanischen Konzil,* Band 5, Freiburg, Basel, Wien, 2009. Also, BEATE EICHINGER (), *„50 Jahre Vatikanum II"*: Zentrale Veranstaltungen und Tipps für lokale Aktionen – vorbereitet und ausgearbeitet von der KEB in Bistum Regensburg e.V mit ihren KooperationspartnerInnen, 10.Oktober 2011.

Chapter One

Introduction

In this research work, we intend to take our exploration to a level of what we choose to call *beyond (prophetic) witnessing* – a rather new way of humanizing our world today. As it is the case, a true praxis of 'witnessing beyond' is what one sees clearly in the personality of Jesus Christ – who is truly God and Man (prototype-human). His entire life on earth was a clear encapsulation of how to free human persons from the shackles of slavery of 'political entanglement of playing guitar while Rome is on fire' (quipping with distributing bread and handouts – while the two-third of world-humans are dying of hunger and poverty). Christ's mission of 'humanizing' the human world was clear from the beginning. In other words to be truly Christ was to truly bear witness to the Father *par excellence* – and that was clearly his mission. As he said, "For I have come down from Heaven not to do my will but to do the will of Him who sent me (Jn. 6.38). *A fortiori* not to witness is to be 'un-christ-like' which would simply be a contradiction in terms – meaning in essence that this quality or 'un-christ-like-ness" would simply be inimically to the personality of Jesus Christ, to his quintessence as God come to our human earth and abode. In the same vein, to be a Christian and not to witness for Christ on earth would be truly an aberration of 'the Christ-like-ness of our truly human image and likeness that has it's fullness in the personality of Christ. Thus in the personality of Christ we notice that witnessing permeates and encompasses every aspect of his life. In sum, *to be Christ (Christ – ian)* is to truly witness to the truth of the Gospel and it's entire implications in concrete (Luke 9: 23–24; Matt 10:38–39), but much more than that; because the Christ of witnessing was equally the Christ that devoted much more time in true, silence and devotional prayer (Luke. 5:16).

In other words, we see in the personality of Christ, Faith – prayer – life (*Glaude*, German word for 'Believe') being realized in Hope (*Hoffnung*, German Word for 'Hope') – hope as promised as concretely in the action of giving (*Liebe*, German word for 'Love'). These three qualities: *Glaude* – Believe (you pray as you believe), *Hoffnung* – Hope (on what is not) and Love – *Liebe* (love others as yourself…including your enemy} are essential qualities for witnessing and living a life beyond witnessing in concrete as encapsulated in the personality of Jesus Christ and as a way of humanising the human world truly today beyond the shenanigan of 'world-politics of humanitarianism' that sneers at true love of witnessing and witnessing really *beyond*.

In this sense we have to realize here from the onset that this work is not another 'manifesto' on liberation theology nor does it intend to be one. But an effort in reclaiming the quintessence of what true witnessing is in the light of combining 'true activism with comtemplativism' – a clear case of Mother Teresa of Calcutta as against the modern and postmodern day 'dry-politics of humanitarianism and mere *philanthropism*'.

And so in this work we intend to accomplish our pursuance via Seven Chapters. In the first Chapter we intend to state the case of the matter in question – the disenchantment of separating action from prayers or prayers from action: active life from contemplative life and vice-versa.

1.1 Stating the case

The same devotional attitude of Jesus in the Scriptures was emulated and lived by Mother Teresa of Calcutta, as she writes, "If we pray – we will believe. If we believe – we will love. If we love – we will serve. Only then will we put our love for God into action, through service to Christ in the distressing disguise of the poor."[4] In the same vein Benedict XVI attests that there was no clear separation between the life of prayer, loving ones neighbor vis-à-vis Charity in the life of Mother Teresa of Calcutta. In other words in her, just like Christ we see contemplative and active lives brought together in one harmony, as should be the case today. The Pope argued,

> Die Selige Teresa von Kalkutta ist ein sehr offenkundiges Beispiel dafür, dass die Gott im Gebet gewidmete Zeit dem tatsachlichen Wirken der Nächstenliebe nicht nur nicht schadet, sondern im Wirklichkeit dessen unerschöpfliche Quelle ist.[5]

In light of the forgoing, this Christ-like attitude of Mother Teresa of Calcutta remains a big challenge for today's humanitarian and philanthropic engagements. And most of all to religious bodies and congregations today that seem to have left the inner life of prayer which have always served the backbone of the Church's

4 ANGELO D. SCOLOZZI (ed.), MOTHER TERESA, *Thirsting for God: A yearbook of prayers, Meditations, and Anecdotes,* (St. Anthony Messenger Press), Cincinnati, 2000, p. 86. See, ROSWITHA KORNPROBST (Hg.), *Freude ist Gebet: Worte von Mutter Teresa*, Kevelaer, 2010.

5 Benedikt XVI, *Mit dem heiligen Vater durch das Jahr; Ein Lesebuch*, (Libreria Editrice Vaticana, Rom), Augsburg, 2008, p.154. English literally translation: The Blessed Teresa of Calcutta is a very obvious example of the time devoted to God in prayer, the actual work of charity, not only does no harm, but in fact is the inexhaustible source.

internal renewal 'to serving table only today.' The consequence of such negligence:

> Much disorder has come into the world through the neglect of family prayer and prayer in religious communities. Such neglect may destroy holiness, the very fruit of prayer. Jesus said, "wherever two or three are gathered in my name, there am I in the midst of them." The Holy Spirit came upon the disciples when they were together in prayer with Mary. Fidelity to prayer is the beginning of holiness.[6]

This reason for this stance argues Benedict XVI is equally for the fact that,

> Wer betet, vertut nicht seine Zeit, selbst wenn die Situation alle Anzeichen der Dringlichkeit besitzt und einzig zum Handeln zu treiben scheint. Die Frömmigkeit schwächt nicht den Kampf gegen die Armut oder sogar das Elend des Nächsten.[7]

As it's clearly the case, it's only through the eyes of prayerful devotion that one can really see the poor as Christ really saw them without serving one's stomach in the name of serving the poor or even in some extreme cases 'serving against the poor' in the name of serving the poor as times has been the case with some modern humanitarian organizations today. In this last instance one recalls some allegations that some NGOs have been accused by the Press of using their means of supplying food to the poor and war-torn countries as opportunity to equally push in arms thereby escalating the conflict to the level of no end in sight.[8] The foregoing attitudes are actually real contradiction that smacks of hypocrisy in the light of true 'witnessing to the poor'. In other words it is only via a life ordered and anchored on true and sincere life of prayer that a true and honest witnessing to the poor would be most ennobling. And within such purview of life that one would be able to:

> Greet the children, the poor, the suffering, and the lonely with a happy smile. Give them not only your care but also your heart. Kindness has converted more people than zeal or eloquence. Our service to others should be kind, sweet, humble, and unspoiled by selfishness. Let no one ever come to you without coming away better and happier. Be the living expression of God's kindness.[9]

How would such a 'spirited' gesture be possible today, if not via a life that is anchored on prayer and devotion as the stepping-stone to true witnessing? Such

---

6 ANGELO D. SCOLOZZI, p. 171.

7 Benedikt XVI, *Loc. cit. English literally translation*: "Those who pray are not wasting their time, even if it seems the situation appears desperate and seems to call for action. Piety does not weaken the fight against poverty, or even the plight of our neighbor.

8 Cf. Prof. Daniel Hellinger, *Humanitarian Action, NGOs and Privatization of the Military* in, http://www.eisf.eu/resources/library/hum_action_mil_privatisation.pdf, consulted on 05/09/2012.

9 ANGELO D. SCOLOZZI, p. 172.

a life is in *au courant* with the truth of our Christian baptismal challenge. A challenge that becomes more obvious and demanding in a postmodern era of razzmatazz-publicity of Charity via the media and cheap gaining of public attention by flashing one's offer in the *publicum.* An attitude that smacks of the Christian attitude of 'not-letting-your right hand know what your left is doing' (Matt. 6:3), thereby exposing the poor perhaps to disrepute and dishonor of their human integrity.

The contrary of the above should be the case. Thus true demeanor of *witnessing beyond,* is the challenging case of one of the greatest Christian activists of our time, Martin Luther King (Jr) who reflects the same spirit of Christ in combining devotional prayer with a true and concrete activism – a case of 'living the prayer-life in the concrete existential human *sitz-im-leben.* He writes,

> When you are aware that you are a symbol, it causes you to search your soul constantly – to go through this job of self-analysis, to see if you live up to the high and noble principles that people surround you with, and to try at all times to keep the gulf between the public self and the private self at a minimum. One of the prayers that I prayed to God everyday was: "O God, help me to see myself in my true perspective. Help me, O God, to see that I'm just a symbol of a movement. Help me to see that I'm the victim of what the Germans called a *Zeitgeist* and that something was getting ready to happen in history.[10]

It was true prayer lived out in the concrete existential *facticity*[11] of the *human person integrally and adequately* considered that was behind, and at the basis of the empowerment of Martin Luther King's (Jr) activism and success story of struggle for the poor, poverty, and the marginalized in the American society and by extension in the entire world where the poor and weak were under operation.

---

10 CLAYBORNE CARSON, *The Autobiography of Martin Luther King, Jr.* New York, 2001, p. 105.

11 *Facticity* is a word that was frequently in the mouth and writings of most existential philosophers like Jean-Paul Sartre and Martin Heidegger. It essentially refers to the 'essential fact and *givenness* in ones situation.' The deployment of the word here is not used in the atheistic sense as Jean-Paul Sartre or most atheistic existentialists used, in which 'human freedom' becomes a 'thrust' on the neck of the human person, that he or she cannot not but be free (*condemned to be free* – strictly the expression of the existentialists). The use here is only to refer to the existential, marginal situation of the minority in the USA like extreme racism in which the blacks found themselves during the time of Martin Luther King (jr) – a kind of Albatross of situation for the people then. Of course this situation was greatly overcome with the great declaration of equal right for all in the American Constitution. Narrowly in this use it could be seen to be similar to the use of the existentialists, but only similar but not wholly to the use of the Atheistic existentialists. The difference being that for the atheistic existentialists this situation of the human freedom was simple 'an albatross', but in the case of the situation of the blacks in the USA then they did overcome it with the constitutional recognition of their right and equality before the law.

Chapter two

2.1 A Way of Humanizing the World? Reviewing the popular theory of Jeffrey Sachs: a synopsis of his work: *"the end of poverty – how we can make it happen in our lifetime"*[12]

The main core of Jeffrey Sachs' argument is that the issue of Poverty is as old as Humanity. But who are at the centre and at the edge of the Poverty-question of Sachs? Who are the real poor, the marginalized of the Society? How can we classify them? In spite of the excessive affluence of some, why are most people poor in our World today? And worst of all why are most people poor below the poverty line even in the so-called mineral resource, well-endowed Countries in Europe, USA, Africa and Asia? In spite of human efforts to end poverty through history and by different programs of the United Nations *inter alia*, what are the factors responsible for this unending cankerworm call Poverty that has eaten deep into the bone marrow of our post-modern society with its 'sensibilities and insensibilities,'[13] to borrow the phase of Paul Lakeland?

There is no end to a lot of questions that could be raised in this area of poverty-issue. In spite of many theories hatched through seminars, conference and workshops etc. Is there any concrete solution to '*the end of poverty*?" And *how can we make it happen in our lifetime* as Jeffrey Sachs titled his book?

It is in the light of the finding a concrete and workable solution to this all-important issue, poverty, that Jeffrey Sachs has written this his excellent poverty-practicable compendium on the poverty-question.

Our aim in this preview is to overview this book by Jeffrey Sachs in light of a more Christ-like way of humanizing our world, which is the objective of our pursuit and argumentation in this book. First, by way of prologue, we shall start with the presentation of the Key general information in the book by Jeffery Sachs: *The End of Poverty. How we can make it happen in our Lifetime*, London, 2005. We

---

12 See, J. SACHS, *The End of Poverty. How we can make it happen in our Lifetime*, London, 2005.

13 P. Lakeland, *PostModernity. Christian Identity In A fragmented Age. Guides to Theological Inquiry*, Minneapolis, 1997, p. ix. See, D. G. BLOESCH, *Crumbling Foundations. Death & Rebirth In An Age of Upheaval*, Michigan, 1984, p. 38.

would begin to analysis the book chapter by chapter. Because of the enormity of the work involve we shall try to be as brief as possible but at the same time heating the kernel of the matter in the chapters. Finally we would end up with Sachs by making concrete proposals in what he called in *Chapter Eighteen*, the last Chapter of the book: *Our Generation's challenge.* We would surmise our presentation/reading of the book of Sachs by making some critical remark about the book itself.

Beyond Sachs, we would state our own case in *pari passu* and to argue how humanity could be more humanized through a more Christ-like efforts of witnessing to the poor via what I would term a *Mother-Teresa-of-Calcutta-Model* of marrying 'activism with *contemplativism*.' In our own terminology here: *going Beyond Witnessing*!

2.1.1 General Reading cum Information in the Book: "The End of Poverty...."

In this 396-page book titled: *The End of Poverty. How we can make it happen in our Lifetime;* Jeffrey Sachs, a Professor and Special Adviser to the immediate, former UN Secretary-General Kofi Annan presents in 18-well-structured Chapters the kernel to ending Poverty in the World.

Why is this assignment of ending poverty important for Sachs? The reason is as he noted that over 8million people in the World die each year because of poverty. He thinks that the only way to deal with the problem is through *a shift in paradigm* in the world's economic and political policies. He thinks that with the shift in paradigm it will be possible to end poverty by the year 2025. Sachs thinks that poverty's end is realizable in 2025 based on the following reason:

> The wealth of the rich world, the power of today's vast store houses of knowledge and the declining fraction of the world that needs help to escape from poverty all make the end of poverty a realistic possibility by the year 2025.[14]

On the other hand, Sachs attributes poverty as the reason behind AIDS, TB and Malaria diseases and their incurability. He argues that poverty in light of this is the main reason for global instability and not terrorism. And the main cause of poverty in the world is the 'role of rich-country policies.'[15]

He argues that for example if the USA could spend just 1/3 of the sum of $450billion (that is $15billion) that it spends on military alone on poverty alleviation; the world poverty could be alleviated and our world would be a more

14 J. SACHS, *The End of Poverty*, p. 3.

15 *Ibid.*, p. 2.

stabilized place to live in. In the light of this Sachs links poverty to world's instability and argues that war against poverty would be the right choice to respect and to save human life. It is worth noting that Sachs could come to this kind of conclusive reasoning about alleviating poverty in the world through his versatile 20years of worldwide traveling and experience. Above all, he stresses the role of collectivity in alleviating the world's poverty problem. As he summarily argues:

> When the preconditions of basic infrastructure (roads, power, ports) and human capital (health and education) are in place, markets are powerful engines of development. Without those preconditions, markets can cruelly bypass large parts of the world, leaving them impoverished and suffering without respite. Collective action, through effective government provision of health, education, infrastructure as well as foreign assistance when needed, underpins economic success.[16]

In the next section of this review, we would embark on Chapter for Chapter review of Sachs' book. Since it is in the following Chapters that he tried to expatiate his way forward for the alleviation of poverty in the human world through his lived experiences in some countries cutting across the continents of the world: Bolivia, Poland, Russia, China, India and Kenya etc.

2.1.2 CHAPTER-BY-CHAPTER REVIEW OF SACHS' BOOK

In the Chapters to follow Sachs narrates his personal lived experiences across the globe in the various countries in the world he visited across the continents as an eyewitness and firsthand evidence and concrete way of portraying the 'world-poverty-situation on the ground.'

In Chapter One of the book titled: *A Global Family Portrait – Malawi: The Perfect Storm*, he paints a good portrait of the poverty-situation in Malawi. He does it in the manner of a good Artist, applying almost a type of *argumentum ad misericodia* to the global human consciences. He portrays the imagery of AIDS and its havoc in Malawi; the toll that Malaria has taken on the lives on young Malawians because of lack of anti-malaria medicines. In the light of this type of situation, he says that the NGOS (nongovernmental organizations) can do just little because they lack the needed resources.

Furthermore, he narrates the case of the untold dying of Malawians in numbers from AIDS because as he says, it shows that the world has decided to look away – not that they people themselves want to die.

16 *Ibid.* p. 3.

Although Malawi is basking in the Sunshine of Democracy, Sachs believes that democracy is bound to be fragile in an impoverished country where incomes are about 50cents per person per day.[17] He stresses that the nonchalance of EU and the USA to reach out to support Malawi when it made a clarion call for support; instead the former countries requested Malawi to cut down her proposals. In view of this stringent condition many lives were lost in the process because of lack of "some precious little action that could have been done by the world-community." It is in the light of this negligence by the world-community and the concomitant lost of human lives that followed that made Carol Bellany of the UNICEF to describe Malawi as "the perfect storm."

But it was not only Malawi that is in this kind of ugly picture and situation according to Sachs. *Bangladesh: On the Ladder of development* was before in similar situation. Bangladesh, a country of 140 million people, which had her independence from Pakistan in 1971, had shown that through growth in per capita income and infant mortality rate that a most hopeless circumstance through the application of right strategies and combination of investments can be a way forward to the ladder of development.

While considering the case of *India: Centre of Export Services and Revolution,* Sachs thinks that India is a typical case of IT Revolution: from IT to manufacturing, research and development, India is fast growing. In the light of this unique Indian situation, Sachs writes:

> Progress is hard enough to achieve in the world without being perceived as a danger. One of the ironies of the recent success of India and China is the fear that has engulfed the United States. These fears are fundamentally wrong and, even worse, dangerous. They are wrong because the world is not a zero-sum struggle in which one country's gain is another's loss, but is rather a positive sum opportunity in which improving technologies and skills can raise living standards around the world.[18]

On *China: The Rise of Affluence,* he notes that as one of the world's economic capital with a population capacity of 11million people and an annual income per capita of $4,000 that the country has a very good prospect. China's economy soars annually at 8 percent growth per annum. The Chinese export grew from around $20 billion in 1980 to $400 billion in 2004. All these put together show that China is on the rise to economic affluence.

Ascending the ladder of Economic development: Sachs intends to use the above study and analysis of the aforementioned countries to show the economic gap between the richest and poorest parts of the world and how technology has bettered their situation, for example China. He states that economic develop-

17 SACHS, p. 9.

18 *Ibid.,* p. 16

ment is a key factor to ascending the ladder of progress and attaining economic well-being. One has to reckon with the real poor – those who live below the subsistence level. These real (extreme) poor make up about 1billion of the world's population; the poor at about 1.5billion – make up about 40 percent of humanity.

Sachs tries to show that developing Countries have also their growing Middle class population; but these cannot be equated nor be accepted by their European/ American developed world. They equally have better opportunities but have equally fallen under the same symptom of the rich world's 'fast food syndrome.'

The poor for example in Bangladesh are experiencing progress and development – they could now own mobile phones, scooters – life's expectancy is better and immortality rate high too. Healthcare system seems to be better too etc. According to Sachs, the greatest tragedy of our time is that "one sixth of humanity is not even on the development ladder."[19]

Who and where are the poor?

Many definitions abound – but better to start with what is agreed. Sachs noted three degrees of poverty:

- Extreme (absolute)
- Moderate
- Relative

1. *Extreme poverty* means: the household cannot meet basic needs: food, healthcare, housing and education. Extreme poverty only occurs in developing countries. $1 per day is used by the World Bank to measure the case of extreme poverty situation. A country as a whole is deemed to suffer from extreme poverty if the proportion of the population in extreme poverty is at least 25 percent of the total.

2. *Moderate poverty* refers to the conditions of life in which basic needs are met but just barely. A country is categorized as suffering from moderate poverty if it is not extreme poverty, but at least 25 percent of the households are extremely poor or moderately poor, that is living under $2 per day. Most of the countries of sub-Saharan African are in extreme poverty (and even more would be in this category but for lack of reliable data) as are the countries of South Asia. East Asia and Latin America include many countries in moderate poverty, but also that have risen beyond moderate poverty in recent decades.

3. *Relative poverty* is generally construed as when a household income level is below a given proportion of average national income. Those in this group in high-income countries, lack access to cultural goods, entertainment, recreation, and to quality healthcare, education, and other prerequisites for upward social mobility.

19 *Ibid.* p. 19ff.

In the next Chapter of the book that followed, Chapter 2 titled – *The Spread of Economic Prosperity*: Sachs takes a historical excursus on Economic development from A. D. 1000 to 1800. In this Chapter we are going to see the conclusions he arrived as a result of this study. He acknowledge as interesting the universal growth and prosperity in this historical epoch.

According to Sachs, since 200 years ago, the concept of ending poverty was simply unthinkable. By then life was conceivably all over the world – not only for example in Africa, India and China but even in Europe.

B. The Novelty of Modern Economic Growth: For Sachs to be able to grasp the great economic divide today, we need to go back to the very recent history of humans – the 1800, since this remains a period of Great Economic growth. The economic historian, Simon Kuznets bore witness to this. According to him before this period there was no growth in human economy, but only gradual increases in the human population. In this regard, Sachs tries to show that growth in population has equal effect on growth on the economy and vice-versa. According to him:

> In the period of modern economic growth, however, both population and per capita income came unstuck, soaring at rates never before seen or even imagined.[20]

Sachs deployed three graphics to show that (pp. 27–29):

- All regions were poor in 1820
- All regions experienced economic progress
- Today's rich regions experienced by far the greatest economic progress

According to Sachs what one would infer from the foregone is that:

> The crucial puzzle for understanding today's vast inequalities, therefore, is to understand why different regions of the world have grown at different rates during the period of the modern economic growth.[21]

Sachs thinks that for us to be able to tackle the issue of poverty today, we must be able:

> First to understand why growth rates differ over long periods of time so that we can identify the key ways to raise economic growth in today's lagging regions.[22]

It is in the light of the above that he tries to disabuse the mind of some people who think that the rich countries of the world have actually grown because of their Military might and political superiority as against the poorer countries. Although

---

20 *Ibid.*, p. 27.

21 *Ibid.*, p. 30.

22 *Loc. cit.*,

he did not dismiss the idea of the rich countries exploiting the poorer and less powerful countries; however, he argues that,

> The real story of modern economic growth has been the ability of some regions to achieve unprecedented long-term increases in total production to levels never before seen in the world, while other regions stagnated at least by comparison.[23]

Sachs thinks that economic development or progress is not a success story one country can tell alone, but it is a 'game that everybody and every country can win.' For him, *the great economic transformation* came with the combination of the new industrial technologies, coal power, and market forces. All these created the Industrial Revolution. And this Industrial Revolution had adverse consequence on the lives of people.

In what would be a period of transition came in the 20th century what Sachs would call: The Great Rupture. This Great Rupture so called was viewed as *Globalization.* But the advent of World War I ended what would be understood as European-led globalization. And brought equally untold hardship on Europe. John Maynard Keynes captured this in his book titled: *"Economic Consequences of the Peace."*

It is worth noting that the economic instability that followed the World War I led to the Great Depression of the 1930s and then to the World War II.

At the end of the World War II came the period of Reconstructing a Global Economy. This period spanned from the end of he World War II in 1945 to the end of the Soviet Union in 1991.

Through this historical excursus, Sachs tried to X-ray the 200-year history of modern economic growth. He concluded that during this period that:

> The key point for these countries is that there are practical solutions to almost all their problems. Bad policies of the past can be corrected. The colonial era is truly finished.[24]

In Chapter 3 titled: Why Some Countries Fail to Thrive – Sachs embarks on an uphill task. He notes that:

> Of the world's population of 6.3billion, roughly 5billion people have reached at least the first rung of economic development. Five sixths of the world's population is at least one step above extreme poverty.[25]

What is the implication of this? The implication is what Sachs tries to workout in the rest of this Chapter 3. He notes that extreme poverty is shrinking and it is in this regard that we can have prospect for a realistic envision of a world without

23 *Ibid.*, p. 31.
24 *Ibid.* p. 50.
25 *Ibid.* p. 51.

extreme poverty as soon as 2025. The key solution to this is to embark in solving the problems of those areas where economic development are not working he suggested.

To illustrate how this can be worked out, he deployed the imagery of the *growth of Household income.* He enlisted Saving, Trade, Technology and Resource Boom as the major ingredients to the growth of Household income. This imagery he deploys on a wider level to show the pathways to higher income and ways to economies growth. As he surmised:

> In actual economies, a rise in gross domestic product (GSP) per capita is typically the result of most or all of these four processes simultaneously at work: Saving and Capital accumulation, increasing specialization and trade, technological advance (and a resulting use in output for a given amount of inputs), and greater natural resources per person (and a resulting increase in the level of output per person).[26]

On the contrary, he envisions other ways through which the family economy might be reduced: lack of saving, absence of Trade, Technological Reversal, Natural Resource decline, Adverse Productivity Shock, Population Growth.

In light of the foregoing, he thinks that it is not just enough to list why there is decline in economic growth but one has to be conscious of *the reason why countries fail to achieve Growth.*

His point of focus is that Economic 'stunt-ness' is basically as a result of:

> The most common explanation for why countries fail to achieve economic growth often focuses on the faults of the poor: poverty is a result of corrupt leadership and retrograde cultures that impede modern development.[27]

But not only the above mentioned, he thinks, that something as complex as a society's economic system has too many moving parts to presume that only one thing can go wrong. In this regard, Sachs lists things that he considers that equally go wrong:

- The poverty Trap: Poverty itself as a cause of economic stagnation – for the poorest countries poverty itself can be a trap.
- Physical Geography: is often an overlooked factor. Sachs points at America as a key country that is progressive as a result of her physical Geography – waterways, good rainfall, great soil etc. Not all countries are so blessed and so they suffer from these hindrances.
- Fiscal Trap: resources to pay for the infrastructure on which economic growth depends

26 *Ibid.* p. 54.
27 *Ibid.* p. 56.

- Governance failures: Economic development requires a government that is oriented toward development. Here Government has prominent role to play.
- Cultural Barriers: Obnoxious cultures can block development. E. g. Attitude toward women etc. Here my mind went back to the practical case of the biggest Black African Country in the world, Nigeria where until recently women have not been deployed in governance. But those of them that the Government have given responsibilities in recent times have distinguished themselves in great ways: worth mentioning are the Nigerian Minister for Finance, Dr. Ngozi Okonjo-Iwela and Prof. Dr. Dora Akunyili who was the former boss for Nigeria's organization working against fake drugs and pharmaceuticals (NAFDAC). Both women have done marvelous works in their country and have received series of National and International Awards in these regards.

These women are clear examples to what Sachs is saying about lifting some of the barriers of traditional prejudice that hinder economic progress and development.

- Geopolitics: Trade barriers from developed countries hinder the growth of the poor countries.
- Lack of Innovation: here one has to consider the plight of investors in poor countries. There are often no room for innovation – and that is the difference between the rich and poor countries. The tendency to innovate. According to Sachs:

  > In the rich countries of North America, Western Europe, and East Asia, the process of massive investment in research and development, leading to sales of patent-protected products to a large market, stands at the core of economic growth.[28]

- The Demographic Trap: He considers as one of the reasons for poverty, when impoverished families choose to have lots of Children. Although these problems are understandable but their result can be disastrous.

In another subtitle: Where Growth Has Failed, Sachs divides world's economies into the following six main categories:

- All low-income countries
- Middle-income oil exporters
- Middle-income post communist countries
- Other middle-income countries
- High-income oil exporters
- All other high-income countries

28 *Ibid.* p. 61.

On why some poor countries grew and others declined: Sachs links this to what he calls the most important determinant factor – *Food productivity.* Here lies the biggest difference between Africa and Asia. While Asia has had high rising food production *per capita* during the recent decades, whereas Africa has had low and failing food production *per capita.*

In summation, for all these poor countries, Sachs thinks that their greatest challenge is overcoming the Poverty Trap we discussed above.

In Chapter 4 titled: Clinical Economics. He takes his fellow Economists to task and calls for a review of the training they receive, and the reshuffle of world economists especially those who work at the World Bank.

Sachs goes further in the chapter to compare Economics to Clinical medicine. He thinks that the five main lessons of clinical medicine are relevant to what he terms *clinical economics.* These lessons are:

- Lesson 1: that the human body is a complex system
- Lesson 2: Complexity requires a differential diagnosis
- Lesson 3: That all medicine is family medicine
- Lesson 4: Monitoring and evaluation are essential to successful treatment
- Lesson 5: Medicine is a profession – and so it requires norms, ethics, and code of conduct. All these lessons and requirements, he says are equally applicable to economics. As he notes:

> The challenge of making policy recommendations for an economy, especially a poor and unstable economy, shares many of the challenges of clinical medicine. Yet the practice of development economics is not yet up to the task.[29]

Sachs thinks that there are areas where Economic development has gone wrong. In the light of this he talks about differential diagnosis for poverty Reduction. Here he lists out what he calls a seven-part diagnostic checklist that should be part of the "physical exam" of any impoverished country. These are:

- The extent of extreme poverty
- Economic policy
- The fiscal framework
- Physical Geography and Human Ecology
- Patterns of Governance
- Cultural Barriers to Economic Development
- Geopolitics

29 SACHS, *Op. cit.*, p. 78.

He concludes this chapter with a clarion call for the *education of an Economist*; since according to him a differential diagnosis is just the beginning, not the end of the process. And in the light of this program-design the Institution is important.

Having done a proper excursus into economic history and laid down the basic economic principles, Sachs proceeds in the forthcoming chapters: Chapters Five to Ten to apply these principles to particular countries namely:

- Chapter Five: Bolivia's High-Altitude Hyperinflation
- Chapter Six: Poland's Return to Europe – a discussion of her economic prowess
- Chapter Seven: Reaping the Whirlwind – Russia's Struggle for Normalcy
- Chapter Eight: China – Catching up after half a millennium
- Chapter Nine: India's Market Reforms – The Triumph of hope over fear
- Chapter Ten: The Voiceless Dying – Africa and Disease

We cannot exhaust the study of all these Chapters in depth here because of time factor and Scope. In summation, it suffices to say that the economic progress and development in some of these countries like India, China etcetera, Sachs uses as imagery to show that economic progress is possible for any country in the world when the basic lessons are learnt and principles applied.

In the last Eight-Chapters:

- Chapter Eleven: The Millennium, 9/11, and the United Nations
- Chapter Twelve: On-the-Ground Solutions for Ending Poverty
- Chapter Thirteen: Making the Investments needed to end poverty
- Chapter Fourteen: A Global Compact to end poverty
- Chapter Fifteen: Can the Rich Afford to Help the Poor?
- Chapter Sixteen: Myths and Magic Bullets
- Chapter Seventeen: Why We should do it

In the above Chapters, Sachs takes his effort to end poverty particular to the United Nations, to the Global body, to the Rich and even times using metaphors to make his case as in the case of Chapter Sixteen titled: Myths and Magic Bullets. In the last Chapter, Chapter Eighteen of this mini compendium (book) on Poverty: "*The End of Poverty. How we can make it happen in our time.*" Sachs challenges the entire world and our present generation on how to make the dream of ending poverty work.

2.1.3 Chapter Eighteen – The General challenge of the book: *'Our generation's challenge'*

In summation, Sachs thinks that the greatest challenge before our generation is to meet the economic possibilities of our time. According to Sachs, these economic possibilities include:

- To meet the Millennium Development Goals by 2015.
- To end extreme poverty by 2025
- To ensure well before 2025 that all of world's poor countries can make reliable progress up the ladder of economic development
- To accomplish all of this, modest financial help from the rich countries more than is now provided, but within the bounds of what they have long promised.

2.1.4 Critical evaluation of the book

In conclusion, I find this book by Jeffrey Sachs challenging and a great work on the economics of world-poverty. However, if I was asked, I would have suggested to Jeffrey Sachs to title the book: *"Minimizing poverty. How we can make it work in our time"* Because it seems to me that the project of ending poverty by 2025 as he proposes is seemingly 'utopian' (See, Karl Mannheim on *'Ideologie und Utopie'* – it seems to me to be a very categorical statement! And we know as Immanuel Kant argued that categorical statements are often moral statements, and outside the 'domain of morality' they fall easily prey to being faulted even in praxis. Suffice it to say that this book remains great as it informs us on what we all need to know in today's world:

> The way toward the path of peace and prosperity, on a detailed understanding of how the world economy has gotten to where it is today, and how our generation could mobilize our capacities in the coming twenty years to eliminate the extreme poverty that remains.[30]

Sachs as an outstanding and world renounced Professor of economics have tried to allude to problems and procure solutions to ending poverty. But it is worth noting as Mother Teresa of Calcutta says,

30 SACHS, *Op. cit.* pp. 3–4.

> Das Geld ist nützlich, aber maßgebend ist die Liebe die Aufmerksamkeit, die Sorge, die Man andern schenkt.[31]

In light of the foregoing argument there are much more to the world poverty that meets the ordinary 'massive-surface' problems and theories that are proposed. Much more 'human and humane' and 'Christ-like' attitude toward the poor and poverty are very important in our world today if we are really to address these issues of poverty and the poor and to really achieve the expected results and goals. Because,

> Es ist wunderbar zu wissen, dass Gott uns liebt. Ich möchte, dass möglichst viele Menschen Gott kennen, ihn lieben, ihm dienen lernen, denn das ist wahres Glück. Mit Gott glücklich sein bedeutet lieben, wie er liebt, helfen, wie er, dienen wie er, heilen wie er...Gott hört nicht auf, die Welt zu lieben: Er sendet uns in die Welt, um seine Liebe zu sein, sein Erbamen.[32]

It is not just only about theories and economic principles that would achieve the magic of poverty eradication; there are much more about putting a 'Christ-like' and 'a humane face' to the poverty-question, issues, and the poor themselves. What is our general attitude toward the poor and the 'poverty-gospel' that is heard all over on the media and on International conferences? What are the real attitudes of nations toward these issues in reality? What is the underlining attitude in general in giving and dolling-out help to the poor of the world? It is in the light of these engaging questions and challenges of being true 'prophets of the poor' today that this research and our effort are geared.

---

31 ROSWITHA KORNPROBST (Hg.), *Freude ist Gebet: Worte von Mutter Teresa*, Kevelaer, 2010, p. 8. English literal translation (mine): The Money is useful, but much decisive is the love, the attention, the caring that one gives to another.

32 ROSWITHA KORNPROBST (Hg.), *Freude ist Gebet: Worte von Mutter Teresa*, Kevelaer, 2010, p. 4. English literal translation (mine): It is wonderful to know, that God loves us. I want that many people know God, love him, and learn to serve him that is the real Happiness. Being happy with God means love as he loved us, help as he does, serve as he does, heal as he does, ... he does not give up in loving the world, his love and his mercy.

Chapter Three

3.1 The Semantics of Witnessing

Back to the Old Testament the prophets were clearly agents of rebuking the obnoxious and immoral structures of their times. One recalls the person of the Prophet Amos who spoke against injustices meted out to the poor and the downtrodden by the rich and most powerful (Amos 5:14–24). A similar prophetic effort is what one witnesses in the Prophet Hosea (Hosea 11:1–9).

In the personality of Christ one witnesses the ensemble of the Old Testament prophecies and *ipso facto* the taking of this prophetic witnessing to its highest echelon. Even as Jesus himself attested: "I have come not to be served but to serve and to give my life as a ransom for many (Matt 20:28)." Christ-event for humankind was in itself a prophetic witnessing *par excellence.*

The Apostles of Jesus after the Ascension of Christ had equally the same clarion call: "But you shall receive power when the Holy Spirit has come upon you; and you shall be my witnesses in Jerusalem and in all Judea and Samaria and to the end of the earth" (Acts 1:8). But it is worth noting that the Apostles of Jesus could not at any point in time accomplish this task of witnessing without devoting themselves to prayerful devotion as the basis and strength of their witnessing in word and concrete action. And this position gets its clear light and authenticity from the argumentation of John Paul II when he said,

> World Mission (Sunday) has meaning if it encourages prayer for missionary vocations in parishes and families, if it creates a suitable environment for their growth.[33]

Through the centuries in the post-apostolic era till our own time in this post (modern) era Christians have labored to bear witnesses for Christ in the world, often paying for these with their blood and repudiation of all kinds. At the zenith of the Vatican II Council this noble apostolate of Christian witnessing was reiterated and reignited. In words of John Paul II,

> Incorporated into the Church by Baptism, every Christian is called to be a missionary and witness. This is the Lord's explicit mandate. The Holy Spirit sends every baptized person to proclaim and bear witness to Christ to all nations: a duty then and a privilege, since it is

33 *From the Vatican, 28 May 1996.* This item 5643 digitally provided courtesy of CatholicCulture.org: http://www.catholicculture.org/culture/library/view.cfm? recnum=5643, consulted on 22 November 2012.

> an invitation to co-operate with God for the salvation of each individual and all humanity. Indeed, we have been granted "this grace … to preach to the Gentiles the unsearchable riches of Christ" (Eph 3:8).[34]

From the foregoing the Pope was reechoing the message of Vatican II Council Fathers on the Apostolate of witnessing of all the baptized as rooted in *Lumen Gentium* article 31:

> The faithful who by Baptism are incorporated into Christ, are placed in the People of God, and in their own way share the priestly, prophetic and kingly office of Christ, and to the best of their ability carry on the mission of the whole Christian people in the Church and in the world.

3.2 The Paradox of Witnessing Beyond

One cannot know the spirit (read, the soul) of true witnessing unless one knows clearly the inner meaning and the life of prayer. To be able to understand the life of prayer begins with understanding the meaning of entering into true relationship with God and then with humans and this is the meaning of prayer. This is because prayer is like *a relationship*. In light of this Joyce Meyer asks:

> Ask yourself if you have any relationships that are out of balance. Is there anyone in your life on whom you are depending too much? When you have problems, do you run to the throne or the phone? Are you looking to people to keep you happy, or are you looking to the Lord?[35]

"Looking to the Lord" – is what true prayer that inspires true witnessing is all about. By looking to the Lord it means it's the Lord that is upholding you and inspiring you to perform the ennobling 'heroic actions' that you perform, to do what you do without his intercepting your human freedom.[36] In other words, the heroic actions are not just immanent in or emanates from you, as you as just a 'Hero,' rather, it's the Lord's doing in spite of you and it's marvelous in our eyes (Ps. 118:23). In this way, good action transcends the level of what I choose to call here a *dried atheistic humanism* to a level of *purified humanism in the person of Jesus Christ*: 'a humane-godly-humanism,'[37] is my choice of formulation. Indeed

---

34 *Loc. cit.* See also, The Catholic of the Catholic Church in: http://www.vatican.va/archive/ccc_css/archive/catechism/p2s2c1a1.htm consulted on 22.11.2012

35 JOYCE MEYER, *Beauty for Ashes. Receiving Emotional Healing*, New York, 2003, p. 179.

36 MEYER, *Op. cit.*, p. 180.

37 A true effort to clarify what I actually mean in this term here would need an entire effort in writing a book on it. But suffice it here to say that the Pauline letter to the Philippians's quote that followed gives us a good ensemble of what that lovely theologico-philosophical concept means.

what Jesus Christ did for us as Paul confirms in his Letter to the Philippians – Jesus "…although he existed in the form of God, did not regard equality with God a thing to be grasped, but emptied himself, taking the form of a bond-servant, and being made in the likeness of men. And being found in appearance as a man, he humbled himself by becoming obedient to the point of death, even death on a cross. Therefore also God highly exalted him, and bestowed on him the name which is above every name, that at the name of Jesus every knee should bow, of those who are in heaven, and on earth, and under the earth, and that every tongue should confess that Jesus Christ is Lord, to the glory of God the Father" (Philippians 2:5–11). Looking to the Lord and reaching out to humans – both aspects must collaborate in a very symbiotic way in true prophetic witnessing. This is what 'going beyond witnessing' is all about. As Mother Teresa of Calcutta articulates,

> Jesus has chosen us to be souls of prayer. The value of our actions corresponds exactly to the value of our prayer. Our actions are fruitful only if they are the true expressions of earnest prayer. Jesus wants us to be more childlike, more humble, more grateful in prayer. And we don't pray alone but with the knowledge that we belong to the mystical body of Christ, which is always praying. There is no such thing as isolated prayer but instead Jesus is praying in me and Jesus is praying with me. The body of Christ is always praying.[38]

It follows from the foregoing that if the 'body of Christ is always praying' it is equally engaging in action because her charitable action is concomitant with her spirit of prayer. Her *vita comtemplativa* is *au courant* with her *vita activa*. By *vita comptemplativa* here we mean: "…simply to realize God's constant presence and his tender love for us."[39] And by *vita activa* we mean: "To love, it is necessary to give. To give, it is necessary to be free from selfishness, to have the courage of poverty."[40] In the light of this a delineation of one from other as we see in most cases today is a clear estrangement from the spirit of true prayer which is the *punctum puncti* of true witnessing that has been the watchword of the Church of witnessing today in different forms: in the individual Christians, men and women; and most concretely on the level of organizational bodies that reach out to concrete human situations of wars, drought, famine, floods and different forms of displacement that humans undergo in our world today.

Benedict XVI arguing on the same line of action in his Homily on the 6. February 2008 notes in German:

38 ANGELO D. SCOLOZZI, (Complier), *Mother Teresa: Thirsting for God – A Yearbook of prayers, Meditations and Anecdotes*, Cincinnati, 2000, p. 144.

39 ANGELO D. SCOLOZZI, p. 152.

40 *Ibi*d., p. 153.

> Das Gebet ist ein Schmelztiegel, in dem unsere Erwartungen und Bestrebungen dem Licht des Wortes Gottes ausgesetzt werden; sie werden in das Gespräch mit ihm hineingenommen, der die Wahrheit ist, und werden von heimlichen Lügen und Kompromissen, den verschiedenen Formen des Egoismus, gereinigt (vgl. Spe salvi 33). Ohne die Dimension des Gebets verschließt sich das menschliche Ich letztlich in sich selbst, und das Gewissen, das Echo der Stimme Gottes sein sollte, läuft Gefahr, zum Spiegel des Ichs zu werden, so dass innere Gespräch ein Monolog wird und tausend Selbstrechtfertigungen vorbringt. Das Gebet ist deshalb Garantie für die Öffnung zu den anderen: Wer sich für Gott und seine Ansprüche frei macht, öffnet sich zugleich dem andern, dem Bruder, der an die Tür unseres Herzens klopft und um Gehör, Aufmerksamkeit, Vergebung bittet, manchmal auch zum Zurechtweisung, aber immer in brüderlicher Nächstenliebe.“[41]

The forgoing acts as a stepping-stone to nurturing our effort here of the inevitability of prayer toward a real mission of witnessing. Without prayer the mission of ‘brotherly or sisterly love’ becomes a mere ‘humanism’ devoid of Godliness.[42]

One notes that from the period of the Old Testament into the situation of the early Christians in the New Testament, the lives of peoples have always responded to their faith and belief – a faith and a believe that are rooted in the power of prayer and it’s ability to move mountains. As Jesus himself affirmed this when he said, “If you have faith as small as a mustard seed, you can say to this mulberry tree, ‘Be uprooted and planted in the sea,’ and it will obey you.”(Lk. 17:6). Mother Teresa of Calcutta confirmed this inextricability of Prayer and concrete witnessing when she urged:

> We must “pray the work,” be souls of prayer right in the midst of the slums, praying the work with Jesus, for Jesus to Jesus. Someone has promoted the idea that our vocal prayer together is not prayer. I am sure that Mary and Jesus prayed the psalms together often. Naturally, if we only say prayers, mindlessly, we might not be praying. To pray the prayer means to be completely united to Jesus in such a way as to allow him to pray in us, with us, for us through us.[43]

---

41 THOMAS MERTZ (Hg), *Mit dem Heiligen Vater durch das Jahr: Ein Lesebuch*, Augsburg, 2008, s. 135/6, *cf.* Benedikt XVI. (predigt 6. Februar 2008). Literally English Translation: “Prayer is a pot in which our expectations and attempts are put out to the light of the word of God; it becomes in the conversation with him, in which is the truth, which is cleansed by secret lies and compromises, and the different forms of the egoism, (cf. *Spe salvi* 33). In the end (Finally), without the dimension of the prayer the human I closes itself, and the conscience, the echo of the voice of God runs the risk of becoming the mirror of the I’s, so that internal conversation becomes a monologue and brings forward thousand self-justifications. In other words, prayer is a guarantee for the opening (orifice) to the other: Who frees himself for God and his claims (demands), opens at the same time to the other, the brother who knocks at the door of our heart and asks for hearing, attention, forgiveness, sometimes also to reprehension, but always in brotherly charity.”

42 Cf. STANLEY HAUERWAS, *Prayers Plainly Spoken*, Denver, 1999.

43 ANGELO D. SCOLOZZI, (Complier), *Mother Teresa: Thirsting for God – A Yearbook of prayers, Meditations and Anecdotes*, Cincinnati, 2000, p. 130. See, STANLEY HAUERWAS, *Prayers Plainly Spoken*, Interversity Press, Denver, 1999, p. 24.

Only and when we are able to combine our work of witnessing with prayerful devotion would we be able to reap the untold and true fruit of witnessing which comes with inner joy and happiness which the world cannot give.

Chapter Four

4.1 Witnessing Beyond – the Christian Metanarrative hermeneutics as a way of humanizing the world

The 'radical nature' of Christ spells a hermeneutical meaning for the human society. Thus, "though he was in the form of God, [Jesus] did not regard equality with God something to be grasped. Rather, he emptied himself, taking the form of a slave, coming in human likeness; and found human in appearance, he humbled himself, becoming obedient to death, even death on a cross" (Phil 2:6–8). Accordingly,

> The Old Testament law of love of God and neighbor was central for him, and he gave a new and wider interpretation of it. The Ten Commandments, a norm of Christian morality today, is an inheritance from the Old Testament. But Jesus did something new: He revealed the intimate bond between God and humanity that transcends all laws. This may be said to characterize Jesus' approach to evangelization.[44]

Thus this 'radicalism' so to say has a meaning and an involvement with and for the human society. Clearly seen in this light the nature of Christ serves to underline the extent to which God would go to identify himself with humankind in the totality of human circumstances.[45]

Thus in the personality of Jesus Christ we see a constant call for faith answering to concrete action – "Give them something to eat!"(Mk 6:37); "Go sell everything you own and distribute the money to the poor, and then come, follow me"(Lk18, 22).[46] This was also a constant model in the lives of the early Christians in the Acts of the Apostles. And in our generation it became the model adopted by

---

44 J. UKPONG, "Christology and Inculturation: A New Testament Perspective" in R. GIBELLINI, (ed.), *Paths of African Theology*, New York, 1994, pp. 57–58.

45 K. A. DICKSON, "Continuity and Discontinuity Between the Old Testament and African Life and Thought" in K. APPIAH-KUBI & S. TORRES, *African Theology en route (papers from the Pan-African Conference of Third World Theologians, Dec 17–23, 1977,Accra, Ghana)*, New York, 1979,p.107.

46 E. Katongole, *Beyond Universal Reason. The Relation between Religion and Ethics in the Works of Stanley Hauerwas,* Notre Dame, 2000, p.192. Katongole argues in favor of Stanley Hauerwas that, "Hauerwas has consistently resisted any suggestions to treat the "social"(political) as something added to the "religious" message of Christ: the Story of Jesus is social and political in itself."

Mother Teresa of Calcutta. The consequent of witnessing to the resurrection of Christ were lives are lived out in concrete actions (Acts 4, 32–35). This alludes to 'relatedness' between faith and concrete living; and by elongation, between 'theology' and human existence – engagement in concrete. Thus,

> The experience of the world as *milieu divin* transforms the secular into a locus of divine presence and in this perspective everything, every aspect of life, even work and business, become sacred for those who distinguish, in each creature and each human activity, an aspect of being attracted to Christ on his way to fulfill the world. [47]

In the light of this the human situation remains an environment where the presence of God needs to be manifested and goodness needs to be done and propagated. Because, "'The world' is not merely constituted by sinful and rebellion opposition to God, Christ, grace and the Church; the world is also God's creation, a reality which can be redeemed and must be sanctified (i. e. the kingdom of God); and even in this respect the world is not simply identical with the Church, but rather the Church is the historically tangible and socially constituted instrument used by Christ for the coming of the kingdom of God through the redemption and sanctification of 'the world'."[48] In this way the term the world as a mere 'secular' hemisphere adopts another meaning whereby,

> The term secular must be understood in light of the act of God, the Creator and Redeemer, who has handed over the world to women and to men so that they may participate in the work of creation, free creation from the influence of sin and sanctify themselves in marriage or celibate life, in a family, in a profession and in the various activities of society.[49]

As Paul Tillich gives credence to this when he writes that, "faith as ultimate concern is an act of the total personality…it is not a movement of a special section."[50] More so love is an element of faith if faith is understood as ultimate concern. Faith implies love.[51] These are part and parcel of the day-to-day existential given of the human situation that Christ came to redeem and that he actually redeemed.

Thus from the time of the first Christian Council in Jerusalem (Acts 15) through the different epochs that inaugurated the different Councils in the life of the Church this call for the relatedness of faith to human life, 'from mere

---

47 P. T. DE CHARDIN, *Le milieu divin essai de vie Intérieure*, Paris, 1957, p.47, in J. VERSTRAETEN (trans.), in pro manuscripto, *The Rediscovery of Meaning in Professional life: Perspectives for Spirituality of the Laity in the Twenty-first Century*, Leuven, 1999, p. 12.

48 K. RAHNER, *Theological Investigations. Man in the Church.* Vol. II, K. H. Kruger (transl.), Baltimore, London, 1963, p. 323.

49 JOHN PAUL II, *Christifideles laici*, in Origins. 18, 1989, n. 15.

50 P. TILLICH, *Dynamics of Faith,* New York, 1957, p. 85.

51 *Ibid*, p. 115

conversation to authentic witnessing' has been emphasized too.[52] The concept of *tria munera* of Vatican II Council, that is, the participation of all the baptized in the priestly, the kingly and prophetic offices of Christ[53] endorses equally this need for 'authentic witnessing' in concrete human situations after the manner of Christ 'who came not to be served but to serve and to give his life as a ransom for many' (Mk. 10:45). This historical truth – the resurrection of Christ is the 'story of all stories' whose hermeneutics challenges towards 'faith engaging faith' and 'faith engaging the existential situation' of the people in concrete. This hermeneutics is what we call 'a metanarrative,' the resurrection of Christ – 'the story of all stories.'[54] This 'story of all stories' has its implication for each people and each generation of humankind. As Lesslie Newbigin opines that, "if our model of truth is embodied in a story, a story of which we are ourselves a part, then the only available form of knowledge is by faith in the One who is the author of the story. We are part of the story. It follows that the only way in which we can affirm the truth and therefore the authority of the gospel is by preaching it, by telling the story, and by our corporate living of the story in the life and worship of the church…it means that we affirm that truth is to be found only in the personal commitment to a life of discipleship with Him who is himself the truth. We have

---

52 H. DANIEL-ROPS, *The Second Vatican Council. The Story behind the Ecumenical Council of Pope John XIII,* A. GUINAN (trans.) New York, 1962, p. 28. It is worth noting here that from the period of Nicea Council (325 AD), till Vatican I (1869–1870), twenty councils have taken place: Nicaea (325), Constantinople (381), Ephesus (431), Chalcedon (451), Constantinople II (553), Constantinople III (680–681), Nicaea II (787), Constantinople VI (869–870), Lateran I (1123), Lateran III (1179), Lateran IV (1215), Lyon I (1245), Lyon II (1274), Vienne (1312), Basel (1437) – (disputed?), Ferrara-Florence (1437–1439), Lateran V (1512–1517), Trent (1543–1563), Vatican I(1869–1870). However, it is disputed as to whether all these councils actually took place. See also, N. P. TANNER, S.J (ed.) *Decrees of the Ecumenical Councils, Vol. II (Trent to Vatican II),* London, 1990.

53 *Apostolicam Actuositatem*, the decree on the Apostolate of the laity, Art. 2, in N. P. TANNER, SJ (ed.) *Decrees of the Ecumenical Councils, Vol. II (Trent to Vatican II)*, London, 1990. See also, John Paul II, *Christifideles laici: On the Vocation and the Mission of the Lay Faithful in the Church and in the World,* (Vatican translation), Vatican City, 1987, no. 14.

54 *Ibid.* p.155. "All our actions and rational inquiry are so tradition-dependent that there is no way one can step outside historical traditions to come into a direct and immediate contact with reality. There is no 'theory of truth' as such – no story of stories that would guarantee the truthfulness of other stories. There are only particular configurations of reality, particular stories and canons of rationality, which are themselves tradition-dependent." But this writer here differs in a way from Katongole. The resurrection of Christ is deployed here as the 'story of stories' in the sense that in this 'Christ-story' is embedded the 'story of humanity' – our story is embedded in the Christ story consummated in his victory, that of his resurrection which is also our own victory. This Christ story also challenges us as the fundament for our witnessing as Christians.

to tell and enact the story."[55] This project is about enacting this evergreen truth, the resurrection of Christ and it's consequence of humanizing our world today.

4.2 Christian background to witnessing beyond

"But you can't go barefoot!" Vladimir says to Estragon. "But Christ did" replies Estragon to his challenger. "Christ! 'What's Christ got to do with it? You're not going to compare yourself to Christ.'" Reiterates Vladimir. "All my life I've compared myself to him." Replies Estragon.[56] If the resurrection of Christ is real and indeed it is, then, in the final analysis it must be perceived as acting in some way in or upon the history of the people of God.[57] If Christianity is to survive and the faith of peoples, it could no longer live quite so unreflectively today without letting her treasured narrative answer in concrete to the faith of 'the people of God.'[58] As Hans Urs von Balthasar says,

> Rightly enough, the event of the resurrection has always been emphasized that there can have been no witnesses to the event of the Son's resurrection by the Father – anymore than there can to the act of the incarnation. And yet the two actions are foundational events of a Salva-

55 L. NEWBIGIN, *Truth and Authority in Modernity.* (In the series, "Christian Mission and Modern Culture"), Pennsylvania, 1996, pp. 80–81.

56 S. BECKETT, *Waiting for Godot. A Tragicomedy in Two Acts*, London, 2000, p. 66. This play first published in 1952 by Les editions de minuit, now done in hardcover by the Folio Society London (2000 edition) as 'controversial' as this play is, however, narrates Beckett's experiences during the World wars.

57 See, EDWARD FARLEY, *Divine Empathy: A Theology of God*, Minneapolis, 1996. This erudite text focused on the fact of God's acting.

58 It is worth noting that with the dawn of the ecclesiology of 'the people of God' as drawn up by the Council Fathers in Lumen Gentium of Vatican II, a different understanding and approach to mission of the Church and her people took a different turn and shape. See, G. ALBERIGO, 'The Christian Situation After Vatican II: Phenomenology and History of the Postconciliar Period,' In G. ALBERIGO, J-P. JOSSUA, and J. A. KOMONCHAK (eds.), transl. by M.J. O'CONNELL, *The Reception of Vatican II,* Washington D.C., 1987, pp. 1–2. For the erudite Vatican II historian, Giuseppe Alberigo, the Vatican II Council was essentially, " "open" to the other Christian confessions and to a variety of cultural influences; it also aimed at restoring both a real subordination of ecumenical councils to the word of God and real involvement in human history, to the point even of recognizing in this history "signs" pregnant with the gospel. To that extent, Vatican II represents a recovery of directions – neglected but not abandoned– that are profoundly imbedded in Christian tradition as understood in its fullest Catholic sense:" *Furthermore, this writer agrees with Alberigo that, "In fact, Roncalli's vocabulary "pastoral" was an exceptionally rich term and undoubtedly referred to the highest level of the Church's life. By using this adjective, then, he was giving Vatican II an ecclesial scope that was not solely dogmatic or solely disciplinary but all embracing." *Ibid.* p.17.

> tion, which is for man, and God does not bring about these events without man anymore than he allowed the passion to happen without human cooperation.[59]

The appropriation of the hermeneutical metanarrative of this Christian patrimony, 'the resurrection of Christ' as the base of 'Christians witnessing beyond' is what we see implicit in the personality of Paul, the apostle of the Gentiles and not only on him but on the Corinthian church and in fact on all believers.[60] This metaphor or metanarrative is developed further in the Pauline concept of reconciliation through the God's saving work in Christ, through His resurrection in which He now reconciled humanity back to God, which challenges Christians to a fellowship in witnessing in the concrete. According to Seyoon Kim,

> Pauline metaphor or metanarrative of reconciliation grew out of his own theological reflections on his Damascus road conversion experience, in which for Paul through Christ's atonement via His death and completed in his resurrection we are reconciled to God, as by His Eucharistic saying about the blood of the covenant poured out for the forgiveness of sins.[61]

Accordingly, if the above thesis is correct, the way in which Paul developed this biblical metaphor or metanarrative has a paradigmatic significance for our theologizing today. For each people and personal experiences of encounter with the risen Christ either through the 'missionary Christianity' or otherwise, challenge to a deeper integration of these experiences, of making it ones own within one's context that which has been wrought for all humanity, the victory of Christ's resurrection.[62]

The truth of the matter is that this 'apostolic kerygma', the resurrection metanarrative will have to be interpreted by means of a new category drawn from a people's experience, thereby making the kerygma more relevant to our situation today as a people of God.[63] Theology so understood this way too, becomes a link to praxis, fulfils a prophetic function insofar as it interprets historical events of a people with the intention of revealing and proclaiming their profound meaning. Accordingly, the hermeneutics of the resurrection of Christ consists especially in making the

59 H. Urs von BALTHASAR, *Mysterium Paschale: The Mystery of Easter*, AIDAN NICHOLS (translated), Michigan, 1990, p.249.

60 See, R. BIERINGER, "Death and Resurrection of Christ. Effects on all" in Notes on Pauline interaction with the Corinthians, (part III, V), Leuven, *unpublished lecture notes,* 2001. The meaning of the resurrection of Christ could be read into the Pauline corpus especially, 2Cor 5:14–21. The effect of this is not only on the personality of Paul but also on the Corinthians, on all.

61 S. KIM, "God Reconciled His Enemy to Himself: The Origin of Paul's Concept of Reconciliation" in RICHARD N. LONGENECKER (edited), *The Road from Damascus. The Impact of Paul's Conversion on His life, Thought, and Ministry*, Michigan, Cambridge, 1997, pp. 102, 122. According to Kim, "In this way, the metaphor of reconciliation, which is one of the most significant categories of preaching the gospel of Christ, came into being." *Ibid.* p.123.

62 OKUMA, *Towards an African Theology*, pp. 83–84.

63 S. KIM, *Loc. cit.*

world a better place and making Christians at home in the church and in the world. Only in this way can one be able to discover what the resurrection of Christ means to a people and their existential situation.[64]

Here we have a theology that answers to a people's *existential engagement*.[65] Which is made possible courtesy of the 'world of the biblical metanarrative'. In this way the 'hermeneutics of biblical metanarratives' perspective has double influence that of integration, stimulation and critical functions on one hand, on the other that of motivating the role of a people to give answer to their faith in concrete.[66] Accordingly as a specifically poetic 'world' the biblical text generates a metamorphosis in its readers, which enables them (and their communities) to interpret their lives in a new light. In the words of Vaclav Havel this responsibility is "the pen with which we write the story of the world's new creation in the history of being." Accordingly, 'the biblical poesis has this possibility for the development of an imaginative space for experiments of thought in concrete.[67] This is *au courant* with the fact that biblical imagination influences concrete acts as "first laboratories".[68] Such an imagination enables Christians, a people to look at the world and at life through his or her eyes (*voir comme*) and it enables them also to discover new ways of being and new models of action (*agir comme*). When a people have identified themselves imaginatively with Christ's resurrection, they can transform the 'self' into a 'christomorphic self'.[69] This has nothing to do with servile imitation or a mimesis as

---

64 G. GUTIERREZ, *A Theology of Liberation*, London, 1978, p.11. Here Gutierrez reflects the idea of Schillebeeckx. See also, P. RICOEUR, *Hermeneutics and the Human Sciences*, edited and translated by. J. B. Thompson, Cambridge, 1980, p.1. "The nature of language and meaning, of action, interpretation and subjectivity, are issues of increasing concern to a wide range of contemporary disciplines."

65 J. VERSTRAETEN, *Beyond Business Ethics: Leadership, Spirituality and the Quest for Meaning*, Unpublished lecture, Leuven, 2000, p.8 "The experience of the world as milieu divin transforms the secular into a locus of divine presence and in this perspective everything, every aspect of life, even work and business, become sacred for those who distinguish, in each creature and each human activity, an aspect of being attracted to the fulfillment of the world."

66 J. VERSTRAETEN, The "'World' of the Bible as Meta-Ethical Framework of Meaning for Ethics: An Interpretation," in HENDRIK M. VROOM & JERALD D. GORT (eds.), *Holy Scriptures in Judaism, Christianity and Islam. Hermeneutics, Values and Society,* Amsterdam/Atlanta, 1997, p. 139.

67 VERSTRAETEN, The "'World' of the Bible..."*Ibid.* p.143.

68 P. RICOEUR, *Soi-même comme un autre (l'ordre philosophique)*, Paris 1990, pp. 167, 200. See especially, P. RICOEUR, *Time and Narrative* (3 Volumes), KATHLEEN McLaughlin & DAVID PELLAUER (translated), Chicago, 1984–1988. Here Ricouer develops most formidable philosophical arguments for narratives.

69 VERSTRAETEN, *Op. cit.* 144. See also, LAWRENCE BOADT & MARK S. SMITH (eds.), *Imagery and Imagination in Biblical Essays in Honor of Aloysius Fitzgerald,* F. S. C. (The Catholic Biblical Quarterly Monograph, Series 32), Washington, 2000. Although this text is

described by René Girard.[70] Instead, this hermeneutical metanarrative reaches out into an imaginatively mediated mystical 'acting as they would' leading not only to a radicalization and humanization of their Christian attitudes, but also to an acceptance of the scandal of the cross that led to the resurrection of Christ, epitomized in self-sacrificing love that challenges a people.

It is paradoxical to say that Vatican II Council, the 'ecumenical Council'[71] par excellence gave priority of place to biblical narratives and metaphors as hermeneutical foundations in her 16 documents.[72] Foremost ecclesial theologians like Augustine,[73] Don Scotus, Peter Abelard, Thomas Aquinas, and later ones like Karl Rahner,[74] Karl Barth,[75] M-D Chenu, Yves Congar,[76] Gerard Philips,[77] Hans Urs von Balthasar,[78] Edward Schillebeeckx,[79] Joseph Cardinal Ratzinger,[80]

---

essentially concerned with collections that deal with the Old Testament books, however it gives clue as to the power of imagery and imagination in the biblical literature.

70 See, René Girard, *Le bouc émissaire*, Paris, 1982.

71 Y. CONGAR, "A Last look at the Council" in *Vatican II by Those Who Were There,* ALBERIC STACPOLE(ed), London, 1986, p.344. "The Second Vatican Council was an ecumenical Council in the technical sense of the word. It was also open to the other two forms of ecumenicity in its dynamic understanding of the Church. This is clear from a reading of the very first lines of *Lumen Gentium*, its chapter on the People of God, its idea of the Church as the 'sacrament of Salvation' and the words subsist in that occur in section 8 of the text. These words affirm the authenticity of the Roman Catholic Church of Christ and the Apostles without devaluing the obviously different ecclesial quality of the other Christian Communion."

72 See, N. P. TANNER, S. J., (ed.) *Decrees of the Ecumenical Councils*, Vol. II (Trent to Vatican II), London, 1990. Especially the document, Dei Verbum, the Dogmatic Constitution on Divine Revelation. While the Church had historically laid credence to tradition and authority of the Scriptures in teaching, it is equally arguable as to whether the Protestant Reformation and her focus on Solus Scriptura that partly inaugurated the Council of Trent had heightened this endeavor in the following period, the so called 'Catholic counter-Reformation.' However, the Second Vatican II remains the Church's foremost effort to rediscovery of her patrimony of the Scriptures and biblical hermeneutics in teaching.

73 See, ALLAN D. FITZGERALD, O. S. A. (ed), *Augustine Through the Ages: An Encyclopedia,* Michigan, Cambridge, 1999.

74 K. RAHNER, *Theological Investigations: Man in the Church*, vol. 11, K-H, KRUGER, (translated), Baltimore, London, 1963.

75 See, MUELLER DAVID. L. *Foundation of Karl Barth's Doctrine of Reconciliation, Jesus Christ Crucified and Risen* (Toronto Studies in Theology, 54), 1991.

76 Y. M-J. CONGAR, *Jalons pour une théologie du laïcat, Unam Sanctam 23*, Paris, 1953.

77 G. PHILIPS, *The Role of the Laity in the Church*, J. R. GILBERT and J. W. MOUDRY (trans.), Cork, 1955.

78 H. Urs von BALTHASAR, *Mysterium Paschale: The Mystery of Easter*, AIDAN NICHOLS (translated), Michigan, 1990.

79 E. SCHILLEBEECKX, *Christ: The Experience of Jesus As Lord*, JOHN BOWDEN (translated), New York, 1989.

80 JOSEPH KARDINAL RATZINGER, *Salz der Erde. Christentum und Katholische Kirche an der Jahrtausendwende Ein Gesprach mit Peter Seewald,* Stuttgart, 1998.

Gustav Gutierrez,[81] Jon Sobrino,[82] Leonardo Boff,[83] John Milbank,[84] John Hick and Paul Knitter,[85] Gavin D'Costa[86] and a host of others, submitted to some kind of biblical hermeneutical narratives in their theologies.[87]

The effort here is not opting for 'pluralism' in the way Panikkar and his supporters would argue.[88] However our effort is geared toward a hermeneutics for authentic witnessing in concrete and making the faith more integral in people's existential situation. For this writer, the hermeneutical metanarrative of the resurrection of Christ is most august for Christians today to answer authentically to the content of their Christian convictions and for witnessing for the faith in concrete and beyond.

4.3 The historical backbone of witnessing beyond

Prayer has been at the basis and the true strength of the Church in true witnessing through the ages till now. That of our generation must not be different, as it seems

81 G. GUTIERREZ, *A Theology of Liberation*, London, 1978.

82 J. SOBRINO, *The Principle of Mercy. Taking the Crucified People from the Cross,* New York, 1984.

83 L. BOFF, *Jesus Christ Liberator. A Critical Christology for Our Time*, New York, 1981, p. 7ff. In this text he handles among other things the conflicting theories on the Christ of faith and the Historical Jesus.

84 JOHN MILBANK, *Theology and Social Theory,* Cambridge, 1991. In this work, Milbank straddles the issues and debates of postmodernity in a highly idiosyncratic reading of Western civilization.

85 JOHN HICK AND PAUL KNITTTER (eds.), *The Myth of Christian Uniqueness: Toward a Pluralistic Theology of Religions*, New York, 1987.

86 GAVIN D'COSTA (ed.), *Christian Uniqueness Reconsidered: The Myth of a Pluralistic Theology of Religions,* New York, 1990, p. x. This second volume rejects the notion of a pluralistic theology and explores whether "Christian claims concerning uniqueness (are) coherent and sustainable and even illuminated in making sense of religious plurality." Of course this book was in response to a former collection edited by, JOHN HICK AND PAUL KNITTTER (eds.), *The Myth of Christian Uniqueness: Toward a Pluralistic Theology of Religions,* New York, 1987, p.viii. this text focused on a "move away from insistence on the superiority or finality of Christ and Christianity toward recognition of the independent validity of other ways."

87 E. KATONGOLE, *Beyond Universal Reason. The Relation between Religion and Ethics in the Work of Stanley Hauerwas*, Indiana, 2000, p.105. "Within theology, "narrative theology" has been characterized by the same wide and nouniform (sic) appeal to narrative, ranging from an explication of religion in human experience in general to the use of narrative as a heuristic category for explicating the basic substance of Christian theology, from focus on biography (and even autobiography) as a way of displaying Christian convictions to a hermeneutics of biblical narrative." See, MICHAEL GOLDBERG, *Theology and Narrative: A critical Introduction,* Nashville, 1982. This text is a good introduction to the trends of narrative theology.

88 R. PANIKKAR, "The Jordan, the Tiber and the Ganges," in JOHN HICK AND PAUL KNITTTER (eds.), *Op. cit.* p.109.

to be the case today. As Benedict VXI writes, “If we take one last look back over the whole of the prayer for unity, we can say that the founding of the Church takes places during the passage, even though the world Church does not appear. For what else is the Church, if not the community of disciples who receive their unity through faith in Jesus Christ as the one sent by the Father and are drawn into Jesus' mission to lead the world toward the recognition of God – and in this way to redeem it? The Church is born from Jesus' prayer. But his prayer is more than words; it is the act by which he “sanctifies” himself for the life of the world. We can also put it the other way around: in this prayer, the cruel event of the Cross becomes “word,” it becomes the Feast of Atonement between God and the world. From here the Church emerges as the community of those who believe in Christ on the strength of the Apostles' word (cf. 17:20).”[89] As Benedict XVI argues further in his native language (German),

> Die Nächstenliebe, die zuallererst Sorge um die Gerechtigkeit ist, ist der Prüfstein des Glaubens und der Gottesliebe. Wenn alle von Gott her denken und leben, dann werden wir gleich, und dann werden wir frei, und dann entsteht die wahre Geschwisterlichkeit.[90]

On the contrary, today some Christians, theologians, and so called pundits have *bastardized* this historical background of true ‘witnessing beyond’ – the meaning of prayer and ‘spirituality’ in the Church, to simply mean ‘extreme activism’ – simplified as just an involvement in distributing bread and clothes to the so called poor. Of course, all honest and progressive human persons know that these ‘handouts’ have not bettered the situation of the ‘real-poor’. Instead they have ‘made more poor’ because these giving of bread and clothing do not really empower them, but simply impoverish them forever.[91] Instead of showing them how to fish and letting them fend for their lives. Or alternatively through a way of helping to prevent the shipment of arms to fight wars that make these so called poor refugees in their own countries. Or more concretely by way of helping their governments to curb corruption by refusing to admit stolen wealth in their country as Britain have done against the Nigerian former Governor of Delta State, James Ibori.[92] The contrary seems to be the case, most of those concerned pre-

89 JOEPH RATZINGER, POPE BENEDICT XVI, *Jesus of Nazareth – Holy Week: From the Entrance into the Jerusalem to the Resurrection,* San Francisco, pp. 101–102.

90 Benedikt XVI, *Mit dem heiligen Vater durch das Jahr; Ein Lesebuch*, (Libreria Editrice Vaticana, Rom), p. 198.

91 Cf. DAMBISA MOYO, *Dead Aid: Why Aid Is Not Working and How There Is a Better Way for Africa*, Farrar, Straus and Giroux, 2009. See also, WILLIAM EASTERLY, *The White Man's Burden: Why the West's Efforts to Aid the Rest Have Done So Much Ill and So Little Good, Penguin Books,* 2007.

92 See, http://www.guardian.co.uk/global-development/2012/apr/17/nigeria-governor-james-ibori-sentenced, consulted on May 19, 2012.

tend not to see these, instead keep on the daily so called 'activism' of supplying arms and ammunition, food and supplies – and letting the so called poor (*humans adequately and integrally considered the deploy the phase of Leuven moral theologian Louis Janssens*) elongate their arms in begging for bread and rice for the rest of their lives on earth. This kind of 'one-sided' type of the definition of 'spirituality and prayer' smacks of postmodern form of *extreme humanism* (so called humanitarianism) that is based on 'politics of power' (right German word here is: *Herrschaft*) devoid of Christ-like principles and attitudes. An activity no matter what form that it takes that fails to give room for 'prayer as devotion to God, supplication and meditation' that leads to concrete salvaging act destroys itself. Such an action in its face is good, no doubt, but it's overdoing and professionalization as it is in most cases today (yet the poor are never *Uhuru*) is simply on its face a type of 'showmanship' – that has taken over really 'religious worship as prayer and devotion', which is what most forms of 'caritative' work have fallen into today.

There is no doubt that most of our monasteries and religious houses that used to be the 'Quelle' of prayers – the quintessence and strength of the Church via prayer have abandoned most of these beautiful aspect of the Church's life and have taken to 'extreme activism' or the so called 'act of heroism' as a form of her lifestyle all in the name of 'renewal' or *aggiornamento*[93] grounded by Vatican II, but which are in themselves completely at odds with the Vatican II inner meaning and true meaning of the Church's understanding of renewal.[94]

The Consequence of these situation is that the so called poor have not really been served; and the Church that needs these daily prayers of these holy men and women to keep up the live of witnessing and encountering a fast changing world is starved of her age-long privileged support of some of these Monasteries and Religious houses. *Qui a casu?*

---

93 G. ALBERIGO, "Vatican II et son héritage" in M. LAMBERIGTS & L. KENIS, *Vatican II and Its Legacy*, pp. 5–6. « Le terme d' « aggiornamento », du point de vue herméneutique, malgré la difficulté d'une détermination rigoureuse du concept, est étroitement lie a celui de « pastoral ». « Aggiornamento » a souvent été entendu comme «reforme », mais ce terme voulait plutôt indiquer la disponibilité et la disposition a la recherche ». It is worth noting that 'Aggiornamento', 'a word which was suspect in the Church as its equivalent word "reform" was still suspect in Catholicism, as the French Dominican Yves Congar learned when his book *Vraie et fausse reforme dans l'église* barely escaped being condemned in 1952 because he had used the word, even with many cautions. But what else could the word 'aggiornamento' mean in John XXIII's use of it, than the euphemistic replacement of the proscribed word with neologism which he did not invent, but which he endowed with the value and power of an emblem?'

94 Cf. GUIDO BAUSENHART et. alii. *Die Dokumente des Zweiten Vatikanischen Konzils: Theologische Zusammenschau und Perspektiven*, Freiburg im Breisgau, 2009(Sonderausgabe), Band 5.

The point to underscore here is that true witnessing or *Testimonium* today must go beyond the mere *'prophetism'* – a return to Lex Orandi (the spirit of true prayer and devotion that inspires concrete action as in the case of Jesus and in the Acts of the Apostles) that leads to Lex Credendi is needed today as never. For this writer it's the only way for Theologians and Christians to be in the midst of the world and to be able to encounter the world of today with all its *sense* and *insensibilities*.[95]

95 Cf. P. Lakeland, *PostModernity. Christian Identity In A fragmented Age. Guides to Theological Inquiry*, Minneapolis, 1997.

Chapter Five

5.1 Christ as the ideal[96]

Clearly, at the onset of His public ministry Jesus Christ *inter alia* indicated that He came 'to fulfill the law and the prophets and not to destroy them' ("Think not that I came to destroy the law or the prophets: I came not to destroy, but to fulfill them" – Matt. 5:17). The implication of this in simple language is that Jesus saw in Himself the fulfillment of the laws and prophecies of the Old Testament. In other words, Jesus' personality transcends the realms of the laws of the Old Testament and their prophecies. He went beyond arguments in the Temples and *caritative* works of healing, to a prayerful life that became the main link and connectivity of his ministry. Phases like...let us go to a lonely place and rest for a while...Lord teach us how to pray...bring to mind this going *'beyond prophecy'* and going back to the basis or the root of the prophecy itself, which is centered on 'on the oiling of the wheel of prophetism to making witnessing more viable. This we might call *'lex orandi lex credendi'* in order to arrive at *'lex vivendi'* of today's complex society. Perhaps this could account for the fact that our witnessing today might be lacking in some quarters to make the appropriate impacts in the wider society and on humans *integrally and adequately considered.*

It's no doubt that most theologians have watered down theology today to a mere 'intellectualism': a *'lex intelligensia'* devoid of *a lex orandi and lex credendi*. This failing link is what this research intends to normalize. And a missing link in most of today 'theologies.'

Knowing as we do that as 'Christ – ians' we partake via our baptism in the passion, death, and resurrection of Jesus – the implication of this is enormous and very challenging for Christians today. This is our motive in this work – to challenge us in today's complex human society from the resources of 'lex orandi' in relation to lex credendi and lex Vivendi. But the question that we addressed in this book goes farther – is the witnessing of life or prophetic witnessing just enough in it's self? Is there something more than needs to be done or needs to

96 Verlautbarungen des Apostolischen Stuhls nr. 2: Apostolisches Schreiben EVANGELII NUNTIANDI Seiner Heiligkeit Papst Paul VI. an den Episkopat, den Klerus und alle Gläubigen der Katholischen Kirche über die Evangelisierung in der Welt von heute, 8. Dezember 1975, nr.7, seite 12. „Jesus selbst, Frohbotschaft Gottes, ist der allererste und größte Künder des Evangeliums gewesen. Er ist es bis zum Äußersten gewesen."

be added to Prophetic witnessing today in Concrete? Yes there is. And this as we said is at the heart of this research work here. While theologians claims to be serving the interest of the rest of us – "the poor…the unlearned…and unenlightened", more need to be seen in the attitude of theologians toward … 'lex orandi'. Because it's always from the former that the later, 'lex credendi' is nurtured. Otherwise, the 'isms' and 'syllogisms' of theologians today remains at the level it seems to have fallen today…mere *flatus vocis* (literally, empty voices) without any *fundamentum in rei (without any foundation in things or any concreteness)* in the words of the Nigerian Theologian Dr. Simon Anyanwu.

In light of the foregoing one needs to ask question or raise the thoughts: our theological forefathers in the person of St. Augustine, St. Bonaventure, St. Anselm, St. Thomas Aquinas even persons like Karl Rahner, Yves Congar were honorable men who distinguished themselves in prayer lives. Their prayer lives inspired their theological thinking and eruditeness. This writer thinks that this aspect of *Lex Orandi* influencing Lex Credendi need to be revisited by our contemporary theologians, especially in our Universities today.

The Church of the Middle Ages and Modern periods were never empty as ours is becoming today in spite of the fact that no age like our postmodern age has produced numerous theologians ever, especially after Vatican II. This writer believes that the blame is not to be put on the Church nor on the hierarchy but squarely on us theologians – perhaps we have not prayed enough as to inspire our thoughts and our thoughts to inspire those we theologize for in today's complex human society. Perhaps we may have written so much and researched so much, but, could it be that we have been 'self-centered' in our thoughts – thinking too much of 'our thoughts' without allowing prayerful life to influence and inspire the thoughts we write? Could our thoughts still be so inspiring as those of our theological forefathers? Even today could we still compare and beat those that followed later, devoted men and women of prayers like, St. Catherine of Sienna and in our time like John Paul II and Fulton J. Sheen? Or have we been much more *reactionary* and critical of the *Church of Christ* – that we have lost the sight 'of the humility of prayer' that inspires thoughts, and thoughts that really touches the heart that reads our words, and inspires true witnessing in the Christians we theologize for? Should we theologians not take much blame for the fewness and the lost of faith in the Church today? Perhaps, could it be that we have not answered our call well as true 'Vanguards' of the pure and undistorted gospel of Jesus Christ through a dedicated life of prayer? Could it be we have spent much time browsing books and libraries that we have left the 'Lord of the work' – that our words and intellectual conceptualizations have become like 'seeds sow on the pathway?' Could it be that we have become too full of ourselves and pride our intellectualism – that the humility of true prayer life that inspired Thomas Aquinas, Karl Rahner, Fulton

J. Sheen, John Paul II etcetera have departed from us so that we are locked up within the shenanigan of 'dry intellectualism' that does not really inspire our simple and normal Christians of today? A rethinking and reassessment of how *lex Orandi* influences today's *lex Credendi* is most urgent for theologians in particular, theology and the rest of Christians in general in today's complex world. It's a challenge that goes beyond Prophetic witnessing for today, and perhaps our best tool for countering and counter-encountering a more challenging and compelling world and humankind of postmodernism. As Benedict XVI writes,

> Das Gebet ist deshalb Garantie für die Öffnung zu den anderen: Wer sich für Gott und seine Anspruche frei macht, öffnet sich zugleich dem andern, dem Bruder, der an die Tür unseres Herzens klopft und um Gehör, Aufmerksamkeit, Vergebung bittet, manchmal auch um Zurechtweisung, aber immer im brüderlicher Nächstenliebe.[97]

In light of the foregoing it is said that, 'what writings and teachings can't do, a humble and simple prayer does…it moves mountains (Luke 17:6). Jesus prayed most of all and he moved mountains and hearts!

5.2 "Lord Teach us how to pray" (Luke 11:1–13): The example of the Apostles in Witnessing Beyond

After an enormous and strenuous involvement in the earlier ministry of witnessing of the word, the Apostles of Jesus realized that something was basically lacking. They realized that the need for reinvigoration. They wanted to drink from the fountain of resuscitation and ennoblement in true witnessing. They requested Jesus to teach them to pray just like John the Baptist thought his disciples to pray (Lk 11:1–13). We must not loose sight of the fact that John was immersed in the ministry of true witnessing even as a forerunner of Jesus. It was his true spirit of witnessing without fear or favour that got him into trouble with the powers that be, namely Herod and Herodias, his brother's wife Philip (Matt.14: 4ff). Of course this true spirit of praying was the secret of success of John the Baptist and equally what he thought his own disciples. This same spirit of prayer and fasting, as was the case with John the Baptist was what emboldened him to face the power of Herod defiantly, was equally the same spirit of prayer that the apostles of Jesus wanted as source of invigoration. But they were luckier to have the 'Master' him-

97 BENEDIKT XVI, *Mit dem Heiligen Vater durch das Jahr: Ein Lesebuch*, Augsburg, 2008, pp. 135–136. English literal Translation: Prayer is therefore, a guarantee for the opening to the other: Who frees himself for God and his or her claim (demand), opens at the same time to the other, the brother who knocks at the door of our heart and asks for hearing, attention, forgiveness, sometimes also around reprehension, but always in the brotherly charity.

self with them to teach them and to initiate them into the true of foundation of witnessing with a success – prayers!

Why do we make the case here that prayer is *conditio sine qua non* for true witnessing today? As Mother Teresa of Calcutta opined:

> Prayer will give us a clean heart, a clean heart will help us to see God, and if we see God, we will obey. The more we pray, the better we will pray and that will produce the fruit of a clean heart. Singing hymns with brief verses and talking to God is prayer.[98]

The essence of 'clean heart' cannot be comprised in today's service of witnessing to the poor. It's not just enough to do 'noble and heroic' work by servicing the poor via different projects and spending, it is equally necessary that one realizes ones nothingness before God. And Prayer-life is the most cogent and coherent means of this realization.

Since,

> The greatest humility is to know that we are nothing and this we come to know when we face God in prayer. It is only when we realize our nothingness, our emptiness that God can fill us with himself.[99]

This 'fill-us-with-himself' is a necessary *modus operandi* for a selfless service of the poor. Otherwise one maybe servicing oneself and ones needs in the name of servicing the poor. History has shown cases of so-called agents of the poor stealing from the Treasury of the poor in the name of servicing the poor. The Executives of some so-called 'help-organizations' have times been accused of enriching themselves from the Treasury of the poor.[100] This is no doubt an aberration of true witnessing.

It is only in the spirit of true prayer that true results of witnessing can be had. And that is why prayer paradoxically for this writer is to be seen as *"going beyond true witnessing"* as a true and a more authentic way of humanizing humanity and our world today. In this sense,

> Prayer is a sacred duty and a sublime mission. We ascend the altar of prayer, conscious of the many urgent needs and interests of others, taking up our rosary, embracing all the other spiritual exercises with great longing. We go with confidence to the throne of grace to obtain mercy and seasonable aid for ourselves and for souls.[101]

How would it sound that the one who claims to champion the cause of the so called 'poor,' assuming the role of a so called 'hero' (to deploy the word of CNN for those

98 ANGELO D. SCOLOZZI, p. 153.

99 *Loc. cit.*,

100 Cf. Unna: Caritas-Chef soll 250.000 Euro veruntreut haben *in http://www.shortnews.de/id/971025/* consulted on 30/10/2012.

101 ANGELO D. SCOLOZZI, p. 157.

who undertake efforts to assisting the poor in different affairs of humans in the world) for the poor have no inclination of taking the poor with her or him first and foremost to the 'altar of prayer', 'to the throne of grace to obtain mercy and seasonable aid for herself or himself and for the souls of the so called poor who she or he purports to carter for? The effort of catering for the Poor as noble as it appears without true prayer life would fall into what one could call 'extreme, dry atheistic humanism.' Where 'humanism' here is to be understood in the light of caring for the body of the human without their souls and their salvation beyond the confines of this earth here and now. Even as the Atheist Bertrand Russell argued, "Unless you assume a God, the question of life's purpose is meaningless."[102] The same goes for doing charitable work without grounding it in prayer and prayer-life. It would be lacking in the real flavour and meaning of 'real charity.'

Since the human person is a '*theandric entity*'[103] as theologians say or a 'composite being' as philosophers like Thomas Aquinas argue in relationship to being created in the image and likeness of God (Christ). Thus any action no matter 'how charitable it might claim to be' should eschew any form of dichotomization of the human person *integrally and adequately considered* to deploy the word of Louis Janssens – the famed moral theologian of the Catholic University of Leuven (Katholieke Universiteit Leuven) Belgium.[104] In all circumstances the human person needs to be treated integrally and should be adequately considered even in the case of Charitable works of dolling out help and food etc. In this way, the complete human person would have been completely cared for as should be the case:

> Als Kernstück und Mittelpunkt seiner Frohbotschaft verkündet Christus das Heil, dieses große Gottesgeschenk, das in der Befreiung von allem besteht, was den Menschen niederdrückt, vor allem aber in der Befreiung von der Sünde und vom Bösen, in der Freunde, Gott zu erkennen und von ihm erkannt zu werden, ihn zu schauen und ihm anzugehören.[105]

---

102 Cf. Bertrand Russell quoted in Rick Warren, *The Purpose-Driven Life* (Grand Rapids: Zondervan, 2002), p. 17. See also, *The Meaning of Life* by philosopher Hugh S. Moorhead.

103 Relating to, or existing by, the union of divine and human operation in Christ, or the joint agency of the divine and human nature; by extension human being it will relate to the divine and human nature in the human person but more essentially the Thomistic concept of 'composite being' is most relevant to human here. Cf. http://dictionary.reference.com/browse/theandric consulted on 30/10/2012.

104 See, L. KENIS, *The Louvain Faculty of Theology in the Nineteenth Century. A Bibliography of the Professors in Theology and Canon Law, with Biographical Notes* (Leuven, 1994; ANL 34) p. 231; See also, F. NEIRYNCK, *De theologische faculteit 1919–1969* (Leuven, 1970; ANL 17).

105 Verlautbarungen des Apostolischen Stuhls nr. 2: Apostolisches Schreiben EVANGELII NUNTIANDI Seiner Heiligkeit Papst Paul VI. an den Episkopat, den Klerus und alle Gläubigen der Katholischen Kirche über die Evangelisierung in der Welt von heute, 8. Dezember 1975, nr.9, seite 13.

Thus an attitude that focus and depicts the entire life of Jesus and his gospel are required for today's efforts at all levels in reaching out to the poor and the down-trodden hoi-polloi. This is for the fact that it is not only the gifts and donations that would make the difference in the lives of the people but equally the 'attitude' that goes with it. Thus,

> Greet the children, the poor, the suffering, and the lonely with the happy smile. Give them not only your care but also your heart. Kindness has converted more people than zeal or eloquence. Our service to others should be kind, sweet, humble, unspoiled by selfishness. Let no one ever come to you without coming away better and happier. Be the living expression of God's kindness.[106]

Such above attitude could only be reflected and sustained through viable prayer life and meditation that is nurtured in the attitude of the gospel as Jesus himself did and taught the disciples too to do so.

5.3 Prayer at the core of Witnessing Beyond

It is clearly stated by the Evangelist in the Bible (Mark 1:13ff) that Jesus spent forty days in prayers before beginning his public life. He often retired alone and spent the night in silence and prayer.

Thus,

> The fruit of silence is prayer. The fruit of prayer is faith. The fruit of faith is love. The fruit of love is service. The fruit of service is peace. Let us provide each other an atmosphere of peace and quiet, which will facilitate prayer, work, study, and rest.[107]

In the light of the forgoing "Prayer is a sacred duty and a sublime mission. We ascend the altar of prayer, conscious of the many urgent needs and interests of others, taking up our rosary, embracing all the other spiritual exercises with great longing. We go with confidence to the throne of grace to obtain mercy and seasonable aid for ourselves and for the souls."[108] In other words, prayer is a *conditio sine qua non* for a true mission of caring for the interest of others. There is no doubt that this aspect is very much lacking in most of today's so called 'philanthropic' adventures. As we mentioned elsewhere the consequence of such a 'holy act' of caring that is devoid of a basic anchorage in prayer-life is 'dried humanism.' It is in the light of this that it is necessary that he who admires this ennobling

106 ANGELO D. SCOLOZZI, p. 172.

107 ANGELO D. SCOLOZZI, (Complier), *Mother Teresa: Thirsting for God – A Yearbook of prayers, Meditations and Anecdotes*, Cincinnati, 2000, p. 50.

108 ANGELO D. SCOLOZZI, p. 157.

work of caring for others should equally care for his or her own soul by way of sanctifying it not just via 'good work' but equally by prayers. Because by being participants in the work of Jesus of caring for the poor and the weak, we should equally remember that,

> Jesus has chosen us to be souls of prayer. The value of our actions corresponds exactly to the value of our prayer. Our actions are fruitful only if they are the true expressions of earnest prayer. Jesus wants us to be more childlike, more humble, more grateful in prayers. And we do not pray alone but with the knowledge that we belong to the mystical body of Christ, which is always praying. There is no such thing as isolated prayer but instead Jesus is praying in me and Jesus is praying with me. The body of Christ is always praying.[109]

The implication of the foregoing for humanitarian endeavors is enormous. Among other things it underscores the importance of grounding our human efforts in the power of He who himself came 'to serve and not to be served and to give his give his life as ransom for many' (Mk 10:45). Prayer at its best shows our human finitude and the finitude of our human actions. It encapsulates our human dependent on God in spite of our human prowess.

109 ANGELO D. SCOLOZZI, p. 144.

Chapter Six

6.1 The Eucharist – as the utmost prayer vis-à-vis Witnessing Beyond

The Eucharist is the utmost form of Christian prayer, because it is the celebration that embodies the mystery of our salvation. *Ipso facto* it is the "the source and summit of the Christian life." (Lumen gentium, no. 11; cf. Catechism of the Catholic Church, no. 1324) It is a celebration of life that finds its realization on the 'altar of the celebration' on one hand and on the other 'on the altar of the world'- *Sitz im leben der Menschheit (in the life-situation of humanity).* This line of argumentation is further strengthened and attested to by Mother Teresa of Calcutta in the statement, that,

> Every human being has a longing for God. Christians go one step further – not only do we long for God but we have the treasure of his presence always with us. We also have the joy of getting even closer to him by receiving him in Communion. Yet Jesus was not satisfied with just becoming the Bread of Life, he also made himself the hungry one in the distressing disguise of the poor. We Missionaries of Charity cannot say that we love Jesus only in the Eucharist – naturally, we want to put that love into action, serving the poor. We cannot separate the Eucharist and the poor.[110]

In the light of the foregoing the Eucharist is thus a life that is equally celebrated beyond the frontier of 'the altar', to something that is much more into the human hemisphere of concrete witnessing – service of the poor. This is based on the fact that Christ is being 'celebrated and reenacted, and Christ is our life,'[111] and the life of Christ cannot be circumvented only within the circumference of the Altar and Church. Christ's life was equally lived with the day-to-day existential-given of humans: in the beauty and luxury of the Rich and in the poverty of the Poor that challenges us all to true witnessing in concrete.

The Holy Eucharist is the *punctum puncti* of the life of the early Church, and every celebration of the early Christians seemed to assume the character of celebrating the life in the Eucharist.[112] And it is in the light of this historical reality

110 ANGELO D. SCOLOZZI, (Complier), *Mother Teresa: Thirsting for God – A Yearbook of prayers, Meditations and Anecdotes*, Cincinnati, 2000, p. 24.

111 Cf. *.The New Jerusalem Bible*, Jn 5.40.

112 Cf. CANDIDUS OF FULDA, *De passione domini,* 5; in J.P. MIGNE, *Patrologia Latina*, 106.68D-69A.

that the Fathers of Vatican II see the Eucharist as "the source and summit of our Christian life,"[113] as we said earlier. It is with such great rendition that the impact of the Vatican Council II seems to be so much felt in the area of this celebration of this sacrament, more than any other place in the life of the Church. Commenting of this fact, John O' Malley, S.J, opines that:

> First in order of immediate impact were the decree on the liturgy and the subsequent series of documents emanating from the Holy See that dealt with it. Every practicing Catholic had to be aware of these changes – changes that he saw taking place with his own eyes and at the very heart of what Catholics had learned their lives should center upon, the Eucharist.[114]

This fact of the 'changes' is not unconnected with recognizing the august place of this sacrament in the spirituality of the age following the Renaissance and Enlightenment periods and their concomitant effects on the spirituality of most of humankind. Thus, as Theodore Dobson reiterated, in the celebration of the Holy Eucharist, we bring ourselves, our souls and bodies as living sacrifices to God – consciously. [115]

The consequence of this is that there is a 'transformation', in body and Soul, a transformation that goes beyond the person to touching every human persons, one meets; it has, also, the effect of rekindling life of love and harmony in the society of humankind and perhaps changing our total attitude toward the poor and the less privileged in our midst. In this regard John Paul II argues that it is,

> Bringing people together in fraternal unity, especially the poor. Serving them, sharing with them the bread of the earth and the bread of love. Building up with them a just world, preparing a new world for the future.[116]

Whereas, every other human celebration may tend to achieve this fact 'temporally,' but the Eucharist upholds this permanently.[117] A better understanding of the Eucharist will enhance the above fact, to the post-modern mind; since, "One of the principal tasks facing contemporary theology, lies in transposing the theoretical doctrines of faith into practical imperatives so that, the theological as

113 *Lumen Gentium*, no.11.

114 J.O'MALLEY, S. J. '*Vatican II: Historical Perspectives on Its Uniqueness and Interpretation.*' In L. RICHARD, O.M.I, (Ed.), et.al. *Vatican II. The Unfinished Agenda. A look to the Future*, New York, 1987, 24.

115 *How the Eucharist Can Transform Your Life*, New York, 1993, 8.

116 *L'Osservatore Romano*, February 26, 1979, 9.

117 Cf. LANFRANC OF BEC, *De corpore et sanguine Christi*, in *Beati Lanfranci archiepiscopi Cantrarensis opera*, in J. A. GILES (Ed.), Vol. 2, Oxford, 1844, 167. Here, he speaks on the mystery of the Sacraments, and it is within this ambient that the transforming effect of the Eucharist is to be understood. But, it is a transformation that seems to be hidden yet, it is 'presencing', to use the word of Martin Heidegger, whose Philosophy, Prof. R.Burggraeve found very relevant to Modern Understanding of Sacramentology.

such will become a principle of action."[118] This 'transposition' is what makes the Eucharist for one, the utmost prayer of all times for all Christians, especially in the light of witnessing and beyond.

6.2 The Logic of Meaning of the Eucharist as a paradigm for Witnessing Beyond

Since the task of systematic theology is to give expression to a particular belief in such a way that it is seen not as just one more thing that "has to be believed" along with so many others, but rather introduces the believer more deeply into the faith,[119] consequently we make bold to say that, according to the logic of meaning, 'the Christian meaning and understanding of the Eucharist goes back to the Hebrew notion of "blessing" as the praise of God which recalls his *magnalia.*'[120] In this regard, "thanks always presuppose a gracious gift which is in fact only real through the thanksgiving, where alone the gift is effective and present; in this case then, the Eucharist is the actualizing of the salvific reality of Jesus, through the words of thanksgiving uttered over the bread and wine."[121] This symbolic act is not unconnected with the fitness of food to express the self-surrender of an offerer, the giving of himself for others, and his fellowship with them.[122]

Thus, the German expression, *Eucharistie – Gabe der Liebe*,[123] for which Von Balthasar is noted, is applicable here. The implication of this analogy is that the gift has its measure in the giving person of Christ (Eph 4.7).[124] And this act of giving is encapsulated in love. It is as it where, an outward manifestation of an inward gratitude – which has love as its zenith and apogee.

Consequently, whether we call this august meal: the Holy Communion, the Real Presence, the Lord's Supper, Holy Mass etc., the Eucharist, is not mere a ceremony of thanksgiving and love; it is instead a celebration of love – that heals and

118 W. V. DYCH, S.J, *Karl Rahner's Theology of Eucharist*, in P. ROSSI, (ed.), et al. *Philosophy and Theology*. Marquette University Journal, Vol.11, no. 1(1998), 139.

119 *Op. cit.*, 127.

120 K. RAHNER, (eds.), et al. *Sacramantum Mundi. An Enclopaedia of Theology*, Vol. 2, Basle-Montreal, 257.

121 *Loc. cit.*,

122 *Op. cit.*, p. 263.

123 NB: In 1988, the work of Hans Urs Von Balthasar was published by the Archdiocese of Freiburg under the above title, meaning in English: *'Gift of Love'*.

124 P. CASARELLA, *Analogia Donationis: Hans Urs von Balthasar on the Eucharist*, in P. ROSSI, (eds.), et al. *Op. cit.*, 148.

transforms the Christian life and humanity. It is the sacrament of the covenant, pure gift of love for the reconciliation of all humanity.[125]

We can not do without eating and drinking in the Eucharist; the consequence of this, is that it forms the fulcrum of the Christian unity with one another, a solidarity that gives rise to an involvement to love and care for one another and for 'common humanity,' that gives rise to what the *Parliament of the World's Religions,* in there *Declaration Toward a Global Ethic* referred to as, a fundamental demand: "Every human being must be treated humanely."[126]

In the Eucharist, by the consecration of the bread and wine, 'we consecrate the social relationships and processes of production which make bread and wine (and other fruits of human labor which they symbolize) possible and available and thus offer to Christ (the true bread from heaven) the bread from the earth, that he may bless it and bless all who make it available, and the entire humanity for which He gave his life; by so doing we make honest 'indirect' acceptance to unite what we have for the rich, poor and the needy. We make a pledge of purpose for collaboration in humanity, instead of monopoly and profiteering; and thus seal the bond of acting 'humanely,' the basis of social justice, and authentic spirituality.'[127] This is in au *courant* with the words of G. A. Maloney, that the true test of how Christian we are, is the degree of our involvement in bringing mercy and love to those suffering: "For I was hungry and you gave me food to eat."(Mt.25: 35–41). We need to hear the anguished cry for justice and human dignity rising from our suffering brothers and sisters and make their burdens our own. What affects others must affect us deeply, since when one person suffers, Christ and all of us suffer.[128]

This inner-meaning and 'radical' logic of understanding of the Eucharist need an attitude and a disposition in order to be internalized as a way of life.

6.2.1 The Paradox of This Disposition

According to the *Parliament of the World's Religion* in *Declaration toward a Global Ethic,* "historical experience demonstrate the following: Earth cannot be changed for the better unless we achieve a transformation in the consciousness of individuals and public life. The possibilities for transformation have already been glimpsed in areas such as, war and peace, economy, and ecology, where in recent

125 *The Mother of the Redeemer*, U.S.A Catholic Conference, No.44.

126 Chicago, U.S.A. 4 September 1993, 6.

127 E.'D IGBOANUSI, C. M. F, *The Eucharist as a basis for Social Justice,* in L. E. IJEZIE, (eds.), et al. *Encounter. A Journal of African Life and Religion*, Vol. 3, ROME, 1994, pp. 67–68.

128 *Mysticism and The new Age; Christic- Consciousness in the new Creation*, New York, 1991, 184.

decades fundamental changes have taken place. This transformation must also be achieved in the area of ethics and values.[129] This disposition for transformation is a fact in the affairs of Men.

This is to be understood as a 'condition of weakness,' without being weak: it is strength in weakness. It is a disposition that allows to be filled.[130] It is,' this manifestation of human life and human history transformed by the power of the Spirit that constitutes the 'liturgy of the world.' Whereas, it looks like an impoverishment and a tragedy, that the Spirit is confined within a circumscribed, narrow enclave of the secular with no roots, yet there is something transcendental in the disposition for this transformation in the Eucharist.[131] This 'disposition' allows for the feel of the human condition, the struggle and the darkness and the anguish, which calls out for salvation – this weakness then, provides the arena in which the transforming power of the Eucharist is felt, because I feel for my brethren (2 Cor.12: 9–10). In the light of this there is an internal conviction and commitment for the poor and fellow human beings.

6.3 The Socio – Theological dimension of the Eucharist at the service of Witnessing Beyond

The Eucharist, which is the fulcrum of Christian worship, throws perhaps the greatest challenge to human solidarity with the divine and fellow human beings in the world today. This fact is analogous to Karl Rahner's description of the Eucharist as including not only a "spiritual movement of the sacramental event outwards to take effect in the 'world,'" (the descending movement), but also an ascending "spiritual movement leading from the world to the sacrament."[132] Although, this unique analogy of Karl Rahner embody both the offer and the acceptance of grace;[133] but in the light of contemporary theology, which aims at transposing the theoretical doctrines of faith into practical imperatives so that "the theological as such will become a principle of action;"[134] and hope for humanity becomes the prospect of theological investigations; it behooves to juxtapose and transpose this Rahner's position in a way, as well as Von Balthasar's idea of, 'the need to release

129 Parliament of the World's Religion in *Declaration toward a Global Ethic* Chicago, U.S.A, 4 September 1993, pp. 13–14.

130 Cf. The New Jerusalem Bible: Paul's letter to the Philippians 2:1–10ff.

131 DYCH, *Op. cit.*, pp. 141–142.

132 Cf. K. RAHNER, *Considerations on the Active Role of the Person in the Sacramental Event*, in *Theological Investigations*, Vol.14, Baltimore, Helicon and New York 1976, 162.

133 DYCH, Op. cit., 129.

134 *Ibid.* 139.

our own living images of God's love for humanity back to God so that they may be incorporated into the Son's *Eucharist* to the Father,'[135] as essential turning points of grasping the socio-theological dimensions of the Eucharist, as a key way for living the gospel by the post-modern Christian. Dorothy Day in her autobiography seemed to have captured this point well; we want, rather unreasonably, sensible feelings of love. St. Teresa says that the only way we can measure the love we have for God, is the love we have for our fellows...and if you and I love our faulty fellow-human beings, how much more must God love us all.[136]

In this way, 'the Eucharist records a vertical and horizontal dimension. Vertically, it is both a sacrament and a symbol of God's union with the humanity. And horizontally, the Eucharist, is a sacrament and a symbol of the human being 'born' to humanity's unity with his or her neighbours.'[137] According to Rahner, if the Eucharist is grasped this way, that is, in the light of the dialogic and interpersonal nature of all sacramental activity, it helps to remove any hint of the magical or mechanical understanding of sacramental efficacy of which the church has been accused.[138] This 'demystification,' will concretely lead to a spiritual praxis. In this way, the faithful re-enacts the one sacrifice of Jesus Christ, not only in the sacramental meal, but their activity also receive that stamp from the salvific deed of Christ, consequently, the faithful now, does not celebrate the Eucharist principally as the *anamnesis,* [139] as that which borders 'on mere words of worship,' but also on concrete everyday life existential engagement.[140]

The supra fact as it were, enhances and compliments the fact that the Eucharistic gift stands not only for the giver and its acceptance by God, but also of the fact that there is a self-communication of God to the person offering the Eucharistic gift; this communion transpires as it where to the persons, the Christian meets in the world.[141] Thus, 'the somatic real presence of Jesus makes possible the deepest confrontation of Christ with Christians and the 'Communion.' '[142]

In this regard, John Paul II observes that the Eucharist brings about a new world, marked by filial relations with God and fraternal relations with people,

135 CASARELLA, *Op. cit.,* 175.

136 *Union Square to Rome*, 162, as cited in *O'Shea Merriman*, 190.

137 G. O. EHUSANI, *A Prophetic Church*, Nigeria, 1996.

138 DYCH, *Op. cit.,* p. 129.

139 *Anamnesis,* here means: 'not only the subjective presence in the consciousness of the participants, but the objective presence, in actual reality in the acts and words.' Cf. K. RAHNER, S.J, et. al. *Sacramentum Mundi, Op. cit.,* Vol. 2, 266.

140 J. VERSTRAETEN, *The Rediscovery of Meaning in Professional life: Perspectives for a Spirituality of the Laity in the Twenty- First Century,* Unpublished lecture, Leuven, 1999, 1.

141 RAHNER, *Op. cit.,* 265.

142 *Loc. cit.,*

Bringing people together in fraternal unity, especially the poor. Serving them, sharing with them the bread of the earth and the bread of love. Building up with them a more just world, preparing a new world for the future.[143]

What is the world without love, and what is love without God? But, God is not 'out there,' as the King, who has enclosed himself in a hidden castle, removed from the human reality:

Contemporary Christology affirms that the Transcend is truly in our midst. God is not to be limited to a spiritual realm, but is fully present to all historical reality. [144] Consequently, the reality of the 'symbolized' really becomes present in the human society. Through the Eucharist – 'the symbolic presence,[145]' the reality of the symbolized – of love for persons, self-sacrificing for humanity, healing of broken relationships, transformation of the world, improving the situation of those suffering from the effects of evil, are known in the medium of 'Symbol,'[146] of the Personality of God as Word, but also simultaneously unknown.[147]

In the Christian the reality of the Eucharist is to be known through acts that depicts those of the 'Personality of God as Word,' therefore, "the Eucharistic worship can only be authentic if it makes us grow in the awareness of the dignity of every person and particularly sensitive to all human suffering and misery, to all injustices and wrongs, and seek the way to redress them effectively."[148] Herein, the proposal of Hans Küng for an *ethic of responsibility* becomes a priority of affection for a Christian, 'It presupposes a conviction, but realistically seeks the predictable consequences of a particular policy; especially those that can be negative, and also take responsibility for them.'[149]

The Eucharist obliges the Christian to care for humanity and to take responsibility, because the Word of God did. It obliges the Christian to the bond of the most intimate unity of man with God and of men with each other, through Christ.[150] In work then, it obliges participants to work for and promote the "bread" which every man and woman needs. This "bread" without which the human person dies consists of nourishment, work, dignity, liberty, love, and respect for everyone's

143 Cf. *L'Osservatore Romano,* February 26, 1979, 9.

144 L. RICHARD, O.M.I, *The Mission of the Church: A Contemporary Agenda* in L.RICHARD, O.M.I, (eds.), et al. *Vatican II: The Unfinished Agenda,* New York /Mahwah, 1987, 66.

145 DYNCH, *Op. cit.,* 130.

146 Karl Rahner conceives the humanity of Jesus as this symbol, which also refers to as the grammar of God's self-expression outward into creation. (Cf. RAHNER, Op. *cit.,* 1978, p. 223).

147 DYNCH, *Loc. cit.,* This view seems similar to the Heideggerian connotation of 'presencing of *Sein.*'

148 EHUSANI, *Op. cit.,* p. 41.

149 H. KUNG, *Global Politics and Global Ethic,* Unpublished Lecture, Brussels, March 9, 2000, p. 2/2.

150 RAHNER, (eds.), et al. *Sacramentum Mundi,* Vol. 2, 266.

culture. It seems hypocritical, to share and commune with Christ our brother in the Eucharist without sharing and communing with our sisters and brothers in the sanctuary of the universe. In same vein, the breaking bread around the altar commits us at the same time to the breaking of earthly bread with our brothers and sisters in the highways and byways of life.[151]

The implication of this for the Christian of the twenty-first is that, the Eucharist becomes not 'mere symbolic attitude on the altar of the sacrificial meal,' but a form of spirituality that is to be embedded and as it where realizable within the mirage of everyday living and human relations, thus, 'the spiritual cannot be reduced to radical internal-church radical community life, which is fruit for the world according to the logic of witness. It requires the cultivation of an incarnated spirituality which allows us to reintegrate faith live and participation in the development of the world, such a reintegration requires', according to Professor J. Verstraeten, "a rediscovery of the mystical experience of the real world as *milieu divin*, as a reality on its way to the fulfillment of its human and spiritual potential."[152] The grasp of this 'other-worldly' attitude and a rediscovery of new meaning in the Eucharist will bring a change of the Christian attitude toward the world, toward life and human persons. Since as it where,

> Attitude is an important criterion and cause of religiousness, though it is commonly mishandled in religious reflection by (1) skewing the anthropologically central variable of attitude toward "feeling," on the side of affect, or toward "disposition," on the side of will, and (2) obscuring different basic forms and validities of religious attitude by insisting on one overly narrow or misleadingly rounded-out conception of devoutness (most often, "faith").[153]

The implication of this fact is that the Eucharist should ignite 'dual dimensional attitude,' that should in fact be seen as 'one-type-spirituality': personal love and social action, the absence of these the Eucharist can be a sacrilege.[154] In sum,

> Take time to think about the Eucharist. God himself became so small that just two fingers can hold him in the host. A small child or a dying person can receive him. The Eucharist is beyond understanding, to be accepted only in deep faith and love. Jesus deliberately left us the Eucharist to help us remember all that he came to do. In the Gospels, there are only a few words describing his passion and death. These few words – which we could so easily forget – tell us that he was crowned with thorns, scourged and spat upon. The Gospels avoid lengthy explanations in their description of the passion, telling us that he was scourged but not how many times or even what the whip was made of. But Jesus understands our human nature. He understands that when something is far from the eyes it can be far from the heart as well. Just

151 D. LANE, *The Eucharist and Social Justice*, in *The Eucharist and Unity*. Catholic Bishops' Conference of Nigeria, 1992, 27.

152 *Op. cit.*, p. 11.

153 S. G. SMITH, *Three Religious Attitudes* in P. ROSSI, (eds.), *Philosophy and Theology*, Marquette University Journal, Vol.11, No.1, 3.

154 T. BALASURIYA, *The Eucharist and Human liberation*, London, 1979, p. 171.

imagine what life would be like without the Eucharist. What would there be to make us love him? What would there be to make us give up everything? I don't think any of us would be here without the Eucharist.[155]

In light of the forgoing, the task facing theology for the future is enormous, that of "transposing theoretical beliefs into practical imperatives, so that the theological as such becomes a principle of action."[156] Consequently, in this 'transpositioning,' the Eucharist becomes, a 'reality' to be lived out, based on its proper understanding. This is my presupposition in this enquiry. And, this is in *au courant* with the fact that, "the only way we encounter Jesus is through a thoroughly historical process. We arrive at our Christian identity through a process of socialization."[157] For the writer, this remains the most august and authentic way today for the post-modern Christians' way of witnessing beyond in the 21st Century and afar.

155 ANGELO D. SCOLOZZI, (Complier), *Mother Teresa: Thirsting for God – A Yearbook of prayers, Meditations and Anecdotes*, Cincinnati, 2000, p. 51.

156 DYCH, *Op. cit.,* p. 125; See also p.143. Here, William V. Dych, S.J, a good commentator on Karl Rahner's Theology on the Eucharist was implying the Latter, on his implication of the transposing of Theology.

157 RICHARD, O.M.I, *Op. cit.*, p. 66.

Chapter Seven

7.1 The Challenge of *Witnessing Beyond* in Concrete today – the case of Organizations and Corporates

Dietrich Bonheoffer in his *Letters and Papers from Prison* wrote, "We are challenged to participate in the sufferings of God in the hands of a godless world, without attempting to gloss over the ungodliness with a veneer of religious act which makes a Christian what he is, but participation in the suffering of God in the life of the World."[158] The Corporate and business world are part and parcel of this *milieu of God* that challenges to "a participation in the sufferings of God in the life of the World."

It seems to this writer that part of the way of participating in the 'suffering of God in the life of the World' is by the way of 'working with others for others' – 'Business.' This is for the facts that in the world of business people work together, integrating and enhancing one another through their talents and acumens – the consequence being that of making and creating a better world for humans integrally and adequately considered. The same good gesture applies to the social and charity organizations. But the question remains how these 'corporate bodies' turn around their 'active' way of life into a kind of 'contemplative' way of life – that is to say, 'into a form of prayer' and *witnessing beyond* in *au courant* with our foregoing discussion here? Can the corporate world in any way be reconcilable with *'lex contempletiva and lex activa'*? In the affirmative, Rick Warren the New York Times bestseller author argues:

> A common misconception is that "spending time with God" means being alone with him. Of course, as Jesus modeled, you need time alone with God, but that is only a fraction of your waking hour. Everything you do can be "spending time with God" if he is invited to be part of it and you stay aware of his presence.[159]

How can one manage this idea of staying 'his presence'? Rick Warren referred to the idea of Brother Lawrence of the 17th Century, in his book titled: *Practicing*

158 Cf. D. Bonhoeffer, *Letters and Papers from Prison*, London, 1973.

159 RICK WARREN, *The Purpose Driven Life; What on Earth am I here for*? Michigan, 2002, p. 88.

the Presence of God. In this work, brother Lawrence was able to turn even the most commonplace and menial tasks, like preparing meals and washing dishes, into acts of praise and communion with God (prayer).[160] In light of this we can dedicate our public aspiration and private ones too as long as they are ennobling to the greater glory of God and through it a way of 'communion with God' – in other words, prayer. Of course this attitude or approach does not eschew the fact of prayer as the 'act of talking with God' in a supplicating manner. Consequently, Brother Lawrence's helpful ideas was to pray shorter conversational prayers continually through the day rather than trying to pray long sessions of complex prayers. As he wrote, "I do not advice you to use a great multiplicity of words in prayer since long discourses are often the occasions for wandering."[161] In other words, "Everything you do can be "spending time with God" if he is invited to be part of it and you stay aware of his presence.

One way is to use "breath prayers" throughout the day, as many Christians have done for centuries. You choose a brief sentence or a simple phrase that can be repeated to Jesus in one breath: "You are with me." "I receive your grace." I am depending on you." "I want to know you." "I belong to you." "Help me trust you." You can also use a short phrase of Scripture: "For me to live is Christ." "You will never leave me." "You are my God." Pray it as often as possible so it is rooted deep in your heart. Just be sure that your motive is to honour God, not control him.[162] Another good way is to practice the presence of God. Accordingly,

> Just as a musician practice scales every day in order to play beautiful music with ease, you must force yourself to think about God at different times of your day. You must train your mind to remember God. At first you will need to create reminders to regularly bring your thoughts back to the awareness that God is with you in that moment. Begin by placing visual reminders around you. You might post little notes that say, *"God is with me and for me right now!"* Benedictine monks use the hourly chimes of a clock to remind them to pause and pray "the hour prayer." If you have a watch or cell phone with an alarm, you could do the same. If you are seeking an *experience* of his presence through all of this, you have missed the point. We don't praise God to feel good, but to *do* good. Your goal is not a feeling, but a continual awareness of the reality that God is always present. That is the lifestyle of worship.[163]

The awareness of God's presence and it's practice in your corporate life, business and organization would help to ennoble a more positive attitude towards humans that you come cross and who are the target of your daily striving.

---

160 *Loc. cit.*

161 BROTHER LAWRENCE, *The practice of the Presence of God*, Grand Rapids, 1967, Eighth Letter.

162 WARREN, p. 89.

163 WARREN, pp. 89–90.

'Meditation' could be another way of reconciling both levels of life – active and contemplative. No doubt the concept of meditation is sometimes maybe misunderstood as being difficult or as something meant for the monasteries or even 'out of this hemisphere'. But in a simply parlance, meditation might mean, "Simply focused thinking – a skill anyone can learn and use anywhere."[164] In light of this,

> When you think about a problem over and over in your mind, that's called worry. When you think about God's Word over and over in your mind, that's meditation. If you know how to worry, you already know how to meditate! You just need to switch your attention from your problems to Bible verses. The more you meditate on God's Word, the less you will have to worry about.[165]

The resultant effects of the above posturing of active and contemplative is that one in the business or corporate life or organizations and all persons who venture to reach out to other humans in trying to humanize the world – would be able to understand "the secrets" of this life that most people miss as result of the daily involvement in the 'razzmatazz of life' with all its emotional roller coasters.

While prayer lets you speak with God; meditation lets God speak to you. Both are essential to becoming a friend of God and equally a friend of humans made in the image and likeness of God in the wider world of mission of witnessing beyond.[166]

For example, the manager in business influences customers and co-workers, and the latter also influence the manager too. In this way doing business is 'intrinsically ethical,' to use the words of Johan Verstraeten.[167] Here, there is a *symbiotic association, as against a parasitic one* that calls for a type of spirituality for its integration and enhancement. The need for this kind of suggested 'integral spirituality' at the service of 'witnessing beyond today' for the corporates and organizations stem from the fact that our world is becoming daily 'too capitalistic' than ever. The ultimate question for money and gain have often compromised the quintessence of our 'humanness' to each other, especially to the poor and less privileged in our societies.

How can the corporates and organizations do business so as to influence others on one hand and on the other hand be 'humane'? This writer thinks that it is within this ambient that they need not only *an ethics (this writer vouchsafes for a combination of political and value model on one hand and on another hand the middle position between Peter French and Velasquez's positions in the ethical*

164 WARREN, p. 90.

165 *Loc. cit.*

166 WARREN, p. 91.

167 Johan Verstraeten is the Chairperson of Ethics Network of the EU, and also, Chair of Centre for Business Ethics and European Studies in Katholieke Universiteit Leuven, Belgium.

understanding of a company), but with a leaning towards witnessing beyond in our changing society from the resource of their Christian belief.

7.2 Organizations and Corporatism:[168] A Postmodern Challenge to Witnessing Beyond

How we understand 'business,' the 'business-world', and its management, first of all is of great importance here? Webster's Pocket Business Dictionary[169] defines 'business' in terms of "*an enterprise established to provide a product or service in the hope of earning a profit. Such an enterprise may be a sole proprietorship, a partnership or a corporation.*"

By way of imagery, business and business-world – corporates and organizations (here the so-charitable organizations come to mind) may be likened to the complexity of the human physiology with the 'cerebrum' depicting in a way the manager *inter alia* the management.

Consider the complexity of the managerial work in such a complex set up as multinational companies! It may be compared to the complexity of the human physiology that sooner or later gets into crisis because of some bacterial intake into the body; in the same vein any administrative misdemeanors could also land a business into crisis.

Take for example, the concrete case of the Japanese stock market clash some time ago.[170] The reason for the clash, the necessary ethics of business where overlooked or not applied well, namely: "Japan's economy has been hammered first by an increase in sales tax last year which choked consumer spending, and then by a fall in exports to the cash-strapped East Asian economies."[171] Thus good timing and administrative demeanors are of great importance in business management. Consequently in the "traditional marketing theory, teachers tell students that one of the strategies for a business to improve its profit is to find a void in the market, fill it, and then dominate it. The advantage of the so-called first mover is again being stressed in today's world e-commerce, but the frenzy for immediacy obscures an important consideration: continued mastery of a market requires more than just dominating the initial competition. It is also essential for a company to focus on trimming an important but under-appreciated cost – the

168 Cf. WIARDA, HOWARD, J. *Corporatism and Comparative Politics*, New York, 1997. By 'Corporatism' here we mean 'Business-world' with single interests.

169 *Webster's Pocket Business Dictionary* (New Revised edition), 1997, p. 26.

170 *The Economist magazine*, April 11th 1998,p. 9.

171 *Loc. cit.*

consumer's time".[172] This reasoning underscores an essential principle in business management, which if neglected may land the business into some crisis as some managers have already witnessed. An integral spirituality that leads to authentic Christian witnessing beyond can be of utmost benefit to organizations and corporates, which will in turn spur them into a positive attitude toward charity-work and the poor of the human society.

7.3 Possible Causes of Crisis in Postmodern Witnessing Effort – the case of the Organizations

What a wonderful time it is to be a boss of a big corporation or organization! Money pours into your lap. How easy it must be to believe with John D. Rockefeller that, "the power to make money is a gift of God" – and that your accumulating fortune is the direct and justifiable result of superhuman managerial talent. The truth is usually more mundane. "The largest and speediest creation of fortunes that the world has ever seen is taking place mainly because of lucky timing, as executives happen to have been around when a greater slice of their remuneration has arrived in the form of share options – the right to buy some of a company's equity at an agreed price, after an agreed length of time. And the buoyant stock market has hugely and unexpectedly inflated the value of these options."[173] In the midst of this exuberance often crisis in business are forgotten or times played down by success often linked to successful 'business bureaucracy.'

Suffice it to say that as much as 'bureaucracy' helps management to survive in business, it may also constitute the cause of its crisis. But how does bureaucracy function or work at times? Business 'bureaucracy' is often like that of government. According to the Insight of Max Weber "the principles of office hierarchy and of levels of graded authority mean a firmly ordered system of super-and sub-ordination in which there is a supervision of the lower offices by the higher ones. Such a system offers the governed the possibility of appealing the decision of a lower office to its higher authority, in a definitely regulated manner. With the full development of the bureaucratic type, the office hierarchy is monocratically organized. The principle of hierarchical office authority is found in all bureaucratic structures: in state and ecclesiastical structures as well as in large party organiza-

172 Z. Hailing, "Time takes its Toll" *in Time magazine*, May 29, 2000, p. 45. Z. Hailing, graduate student at Shanghai's Fudan University won the International Management Symposium, St. Gallen, with this article.

173 *The Economist*, August 7 1999, p. 11. See also, *Fortune magazine*, "On the amazing future of Business," March 13, 2000.

tions and private enterprises. It does not matter for the character of bureaucracy whether its authority is called 'private of public.'"[174] At times bureaucracy runs amuck and crisis sets in. This has often been with some so-called 'charitable organization.' Sometimes the bureaucracies are 'excessive' that before decisions are finalized the poor, the weak, natural-catastrophe-thorn-countries and 'war-thorn-countries die of hunger before aids arrive.

Thus a 'misdirected bureaucracy' in the organizations and corporates could see a retardation in reaching out promptly in supporting the poor; more so, the formerly progressive corporate could run into break-ups: 'Share values retreat, boards face a dilemma; do they assume that the boss who was worth a fortune when equity prices were high is still worth a fortune when they are low, and replace devalued shares with expensive cash? Secondly, even if accounts do not show it, options may in practice impose a cost on shareholders by diluting a firm's existing equity; a third difficulty is more fundamental: an attempting to align the interests of the managers and the owners of a company, the owners have introduced a bias that may come back to bite them. Managers motivated by options have been jacking up their firm's share prices; often by issuing debt and using the proceeds to buy back equity. Another, influential economic idea, the Modigliani-Miller theorem, named after its two Nobel-prize-winning originators, suggests that it is fine: how a firm is financed makes no difference to its value, other things being equal. But running up debts does make a difference to the value of those options. And other things are not equal: very high levels of corporate debt make a firm more vulnerable to bankruptcy in the event of a downturn'[175] and by extension it's obligation of helping the down trodden in the human society by way of charity might be affected adversely.

The manager (management), often, bores the greater part of the risks in this mucky business situation; in spite of the fact that the manager works in corroborations with others, but at the end of the day he or she goes to roost with the chicken with the business crisis hanging on the shoulder. *Quid a casu?* In this kind of crisis situation especially, and indeed, at all times the manager needs *forbearance at work* and management of this kind of boredom. An integral spirituality which is not to be seen as some kind of panacea applied from outside but that which is part and parcel of his or her daily business milieu will keep the manager going. This is a possible and unarticulated missing link in corporate, organizational, and

174 "Bureaucracy" in Max Weber: *Essays in Sociology*, Oxford, New York, 1946, pp. 196–203, 224 –226, in Michael Curtis (ed.) *Nature of Politics*, p. 412.

175 *The Economist*, "The trouble with Stock Options", August 7th 1999, p. 12. See also: Alfred Nicol, "Guinea Pig" in *The Commonweal: A review of Religion, Politics and Culture*, September 22, 2000, 14 -15.

business management today.[176] If this kind of integration is had, managers will relent from contemplating 'alternative actions' like suicide as some have done in history, when their business stocks fall even to the lowest level. But the ground for understanding this integral spirituality and witnessing beyond in concrete of the business manager presupposes a *nuanced* understanding of the world in which business takes place.

7.4 The World of Social Organizations and the Corporate-world vis-à-vis spirituality of witnessing beyond

How should we understand the 'world' of corporates, organizations and businesses – to enable us construe a true suggestive and integral spirituality for them in their effort to be part of the rest of humans in witnessing beyond? We intend to understand the world in which business is part and parcel as that which is 'not merely constituted by sinful and rebellion opposition to God, Christ, grace and the Church; the world is also God's creation, a reality which can be redeemed and must be sanctified.'[177]

In this vein, 'Humans are not simply beings who manipulate their world. They are capable of reading the message that the world carries within it, that is written in all things making up the world. Humans are beings capable of reading the world's message. They are never illiterate with respect to this particular alphabet. They can read and interpret the message in a multiplicity of languages. To live is to read and interpret. In the ephemeral, they can read the Permanent; in the temporal, the Eternal; in the world, God. Then the ephemeral is transfigured into a sign of the presence of the Permanence, the temporal into a symbol of the reality of the Eternal, the world into a great and grand sacrament of God.'[178] In this way, the "world" of corporates, organizations and business is to be construed as a *milieu divin* to deploy the word of Teilhard de Chardin.

In this regard, the transposition of the world as abode of the divine via the breakage of the dichotomy between physics and theology by Teilhard de Chardin becomes of importance to a better grasping of spirituality for this century in corporates, organizations and businesses. John Paul II in *Christifideles laici*

176 See, P. C. Okuma, *Understanding Human Work and Dignity*, Enugu, 1997, pp. 81–101.

177 K. Rahner, *Theological Investigations. Man in the Church.* Vol. II trans. by Karl H. Kruger, Baltimore, London, 1963, p. 323.

178 L. Boff, *Sacraments of Life. Life of the Sacraments. Story Theology.* D. John, (trans.), Beltsville MD, 1987, pp. 1- 2. *Christifideles laici.*

explains further, the term 'secular' (read 'world') as "an act of God the creator and redeemer, who has handed over the world to women and men, so that they may participate in the work of creation, free from the influence of sin and sanctify themselves in marriage or the celibate life, in a family, in a profession, and in the various activities of society."[179]

Seen this way the 'world of the corporate and organizations' becomes a way of attaining 'heaven': witnessing beyond the eternal bliss through the fulfillment of earth.[180]

Consequently, 'the challenge will be more than ever be: writing the story of a new creation in concrete world of corporates and organizations. This story will not merely be written by abstract discourses on ethics, nor by individualistic piety of individuals who seek refuge in the security of a church which distinguishes itself from the world, nor by individuals who cultivate an outer-worldly or narcissistic form of spirituality, but by people who dare to listen to their deeper longings in the loneliness of their own hearts, who dare to make a fundamental life-choice and who are ready to bear the consequence of it. People who engage themselves in the transformation process of a world on its ways to its fulfillment in Christ, alpha and omega of history; People who dare to row against the stream; People who use their expertise so that others can live better after they have gone; People who give out to the poor and less privileged 'until it hurts' – without holding back. The transformation of the world starts with this type of exteriorization – of a courageous inner journey that we call "spiritual life"[181] that culminates in true witnessing.

7.5 Witnessing beyond vis-à-vis the global challenge in Charity-Action Today

It behooves to say with A. McIntyre, that 'what is typical of some corporates and organizations is manipulative rationality. It is not managing the body but now even of the soul' – 'the management of the Heart'.[182] As Fulton J. Sheen suggests, 'when we do not know where we are coming and where we are going life becomes

179 John Paul II, *Christifideles laici: The lay members of Christ's faithful people,* n.15.

180 Sheen, *Op. cit.* p. 70.

181 J. Verstraeten, "The Rediscovery of meaning in Professional life: Perspectives for Spirituality of the laity in the Twenty-first Century", in *pro manuscripto*, Leuven, 1999, pp. 16–17.

182 Walter Isaacson, writing (in *Time magazine*, April 13, 1998, p. 35) says of the Twenty-first century: "we'll encode our dreams and vanities and hubris. We'll clone ourselves, we'll custom-design our kids. The challenge will not be scientific but moral." Even spiritual!

meaningless; we merely concentrate on motions.'[183] Meaninglessness thus, is the bane of success in any human Endeavour. A rediscovery of meaning in corporate life and in the aspirations of the organizations will dethrone crisis and lead to an enhancement of the prowess which will in turn, turn out positive for humanizing our world. How to go about this discovery of meaningfulness is through a life of 'witnessing beyond.'

7.6 Grasping the inner logic of Witnessing beyond in the light of Today's Concrete Challenges

How are we to understand this model of witnessing beyond here? In the past especially in the Medieval period, there is a titillation towards understanding spirituality as 'Fulgo Mundi' – fleeing from the world as a way of achieving spiritual well being. Thus we see spiritual books like "Imitation of Christ" by Thomas á Kempis giving a picturesque of the era.

But still today in our postmodern era, "a common misconception of spiritual or 'spending time with God' as it's sometimes called by some means being *alone* with him. As Rick Warren notes, "Of course as Jesus modeled, you need time alone with God, but that is only a fraction of your waking hours. *Everything* you do can be "spending time with God"[184] if he is invited to be a part of it and you stay aware of his presence. As we suggested earlier, the Classic book on learning how to develop a constant conversation with God is *Practicing the Presence of God.* Brother Lawrence, a humble cook in a French monastery, wrote it in the seventeenth century. Brother Lawrence was able to turn even the most commonplace and mental tasks, like preparing meals and washing dishes, into acts of praise and communion with God. They key to friendship with God, he said, is not changing what you do, but changing your attitude toward what you do. What you normally do for yourself you begin doing for God, whether it is eating, bathing, working, relaxing or taking out the trash. Today we often feel we must "get away" from our daily routine in order to worship God, but that is only because we haven't learned to practice his presence all the time. Brother Lawrence found it easy to worship God through the common tasks of life; he didn't have to go away for special spiritual retreats.[185]

Another of Brother Lawrence's helpful ideas was to pray shorter conversational prayers continually through the day rather than trying to pray long sessions

183 See, *Wits and Wisdom* of Fulton. J. Sheen.
184 WARREN, *Op. cit.* p. 88.
185 *Ibid*

of complex prayers, to maintain focus and counteract wandering thoughts. Practicing the presence of God is a skill, a habit you can develop. Just as musicians practice scales every day in order to play beautiful music with ease, you must force yourself to think about God at different times in your day. You must train your mind to remember God.[186] As we reiterates with Rick Warren once more here,

> When you think about problems over and over in your mind that's called worry. When you think about God's Word over and over in your mind, that's meditation. If you know how to worry, you already know how to meditate. You must need to switch your attention from your problems to Bible verses. The more you meditate on God's Word, the less you will have to worry about.[187]

These beautiful words would no doubt be of great help to Corporate Managers and people in the daily life struggle for themselves, their families and by extension for humans.

But we know that the human person is astride of two worlds, he or she is not only an 'Imago Dei' (image of God) but also an 'Imago Mundi,'(image of the world) to use the word of Rudolf Bultmann. The human person is a 'Personality: Heaven and Earth'.[188] A basic and integral spirituality that culminates in 'witnessing beyond' must as it where take cognizance of this fact. As Johan Verstraeten explains, 'spirituality is not escape from the world but having deep relationship with people and with the world. It is a call to step out of yourself to manage yourself, others etcetera.' This is *au courant* with the fact that, "the only way we encounter Jesus is through a thoroughly historical process. We arrive at our Christian identity through a process of socialization."[189] Thus an integral spirituality of the corporates and organizations should work towards 'the humanization of the world'. The spiritual recipe for this kind of project is that which works 'through the transformation of the business world with the exteriorization in business of a courageous inner journey that we call spiritual life that culminates in authentic witnessing for Christ in the poor and needy.'[190]

Mother Teresa of Calcutta sums up this well when she opines that,

> What is the Good news? The Good News is that God still loves the world through each one of you. You are God's good news; you are God's love in action. Jesus cannot walk in the streets

186 WARREN, *Op. cit.* pp. 88–89.

187 WARREN, p. 90.

188 Fulton J. Sheen, *Christ-centered Wisdom for the Third Millennium*, Missouri, 1999, p. 69.

189 L. Richard, O. M. I, *The Mission of the Church: A Contemporary Agenda* in L. Richard, O. M. I, (eds.), et al. *Vatican II: The Unfinished Agenda*, New York /Mahwah, 1987, p. 66.

190 See, J. Verstraeten, in *pro manuscripto*, "Beyond Business Ethics: Leadership, Spirituality and the Quest for Meaning", Leuven, 2000.

> of Calcutta and in the streets of the world now, so what he does – through me, through you – he walks and touches the poor. Today, God loves the world so much by sending us.[191]

This kind of attitude will aim at hermeneutical understanding of the arena of the corporates and organizations as part of *milieu divin* as we suggested above and with the manager of these corporates and organizations seeing himself or herself as a co-creator and steward of creation. This kind of integrality being suggested here will aim at redressing what Stefan Wyszynski notices today,

> Man is lost in pursuit, driven by 'duty', which he often understands rather as a sense of external need than as a moral value. Moreover, we are becoming the slaves of things. We are so absorbed in and engrossed by the perfecting of what we do that we completely forget about ourselves. We even consider that excessive work frees us from the duty of molding our own souls.[192]

Thus the corporate arena should be 'spiritually enriched environment,' with the extinction of the age-long, *dichotomy between the body and soul*, between the so called sacred and profane.[193] This should be the case since as it were, 'spirituality is not just a state of being, frequently approached through "spiritual exercises' and acts of discipline that puts one in touch with realities, or a Reality, not discernible in ordinary experience. Deepening a relation to that Reality by humanizing the world in which one lives is what life is all about."[194] The world of the corporate is part and parcel of this reality that needs to be deepened via this integrality. Thus as Mother Teresa of Calcutta suggests,

> Du kannst beten, wahrend du arbeitest. Es bedarf nur einer kleinen Erhebung des Herzens zu ihm: ich liebe dich, Gott, ich vertraue auf dich, ich glaube an dich, ich brauche dich jetzt.[195]

In concrete, the corporates and organizations might find the contemplation and internalization of the 'Word of God' (The Bible) helpful as a resource material for an ennobling ethics and reminder of the task of witnessing beyond for Christ via business. As it is said, "only the light of faith and meditation on the Word of God can enable us to find everywhere and always the God "in whom we live and exist"(Acts 17:28); only this can seek his will in everything, see Christ in all men,

191 ANGELO D. SCOLOZZI, (Complier), *Mother Teresa: Thirsting for God – A Yearbook of prayers, Meditations and Anecdotes*, Cincinnati, 2000, p. 36.

192 S. Wyszynski, All You Who Labour: Work and the Sanctification of daily life, Manchester, 1995, p. 29.

193 R. McAfee Brown, *Spirituality and liberation. Overcoming the Great fallacy*, London, 1988, 26–27.

194 *Ibid.* p. 17.

195 ROSWITHA KORNPROBST (Hg.), *Freude ist Gebet. Worte von Mutter Teresa,* p. 6. English Literal Translation (mine): You can pray while you are working. It just needs a little rasing of the Heart to Him: I love you, God, I hope in you; I believe in you, I need you now.

acquaintance or stranger, make sound judgments on the true meaning and value of temporal realities both in themselves and relation to man's end."[196]

In all, the hermeneutics of this discourse could become a background for integrality for the corporates and organizations that answers in concrete to their day-to-day dealings with fellow humans and thus making the human world of business a new horizon for discovering God by extension the wider world – 'a humane abode' fit for humans. Essentially this would help today's corporates and organizations to 'develop their own potential and become a complete 'humane entities' – as opposed to mere tools at the service of the economy.[197] And not only this, it will also aid them in accepting responsibility not only for themselves but also for the rest of humans – rich and poor alike.

196 *Apostolicam Actuositatem, the decree on the lay apostolate* no.4, in N. P. TANNER, SJ (ed.) *Decrees of the Ecumenical Councils, Vol. II (Trent to Vatican II)*, London, 1990; ASS 57, 1965, p. 37.

197 De Stexhe, & J. Verstraeten, *Matters of Breath: Foundations for Professional Ethics (European Ethics Network Core Materials for the Development of Courses in Professional Ethics)*, Leuven, 2000, p.xii.

General Conclusion

It has become almost a general attitude today that most human persons, corporates, and organizations – whether secular or religious have or are attempting to develop or have developed a part of its tentacle toward 'helping the poor' or what we may call here 'humanitarian efforts'. There is no doubt that it is an ennobling work and very praiseworthy.

However it remains to be seen how many of such efforts are really 'Christ-like.' And only really when they are 'Christ-like' in nature that they would truly stand the test of the times and really be 'light shinning out in the darkness' of today's human extreme individualism and self-centeredness. And this is where the question of 'prayer, the Eucharist and spirituality' come in within the general milieu of humanitarian, philanthropic and even corporate efforts in trying to humanize our world by way of 'dolling-out' help and aids.

Indeed, such 'ennobling efforts' for fellow humans if they are lacking in the fundament of prayer and in-depth spirituality would end up as mere 'dry humanism'. Until we realize and recognize that,

> Prayer is the most important tool for your mission in the world. People may refuse our love or reject our message, but they are defenseless against our prayers. Like an intercontinental missile you can aim a prayer at a person's heart whether you are ten feet or 10,000 miles ways. What should you pray for? The Bible tells us to pray for opportunities to witness, for courage to speak up, for those who will believe, for the rapid spread of the message, and for more workers. Prayer makes you a partner with others around the world.[198]

And of course not just a partner for the sake of partnership but also a selfless partner that is at the beck and call of those who you are rendering selfless service.

The consequence of such efforts and Endeavour in grounding our self-services to humans in order to be truly 'witnessing beyond' must come from the Eucharist, from meditation, from prayer: "…if we pray – we will believe. If we believe – we will love. If we love – we will serve. Only then will we put our love for God into action, through service to Christ in the distressing disguise of the poor."[199] And in so doing one is really and truly *witnessing and witnessing beyond.*

---

198 RICK WARREN, *The Purpose Driven Life. What on Earth am I Here For*, Michigan, 2002, pp. 300–301.

199 ANGELO D. SCOLOZZI, (Complier), *Mother Teresa: Thirsting for God – A Yearbook of prayers, Meditations and Anecdotes*, Cincinnati, 2000, p. 86.

Bibliography

A. Books

ALBERIGO, G. J-P. JOSSUA, J-P and J. A. KOMONCHAK (eds.), transl. by M. J. O'CONNELL, *The Reception of Vatican II,* Washington D.C 1987.

APPIAH-KUBI, K. & TORRES, S. *African Theology* (papers from the Pan-African Conference of Third World Theologians, Dec 17–23, 1977, Accra, Ghana), New York, 1979.

AQUINAS, T. *Summa Theologiae*, 111a.

ARINZE, F. A. *The Holy Eucharist*, Huntington, 2001.

BALASURIYA, T. *The Eucharist and Human liberation*, London, 1979.

BALTHASAR, H. von URS, *Mysterium Paschale: The Mystery of Easter*, AIDAN NICHOLS (translated), Michigan, 1990.

BAUMAN, Z. *Globalization. The Human Consequences*, Oxford, 1998.

BAUSENHART, G. et. alii. *Die Dokumente des Zweiten Vatikanischen Konzils: Theologische Zusammenschau und Perspektiven*, Freiburg im Breisgau, 2009(Sonderausgabe), Band 5.

BECKETT, S. *Waiting for Godot. A Tragicomedy in Two Acts,* London, 2000, (first published 1956).

BENEDIKT XVI, *Mit dem heiligen Vater durch das Jahr; Ein Lesebuch*, (Libreria Editrice Vaticana, Rom), Augsburg, 2008.

BLOESCH, D. G. *Crumbling Foundations. Death & Rebirth In An Age of Upheaval*, Michigan, 1984.

BIERINGER, R. "Death and Resurrection of Christ. Effects on all" in Notes on Pauline interaction with the Corinthians, (part III, V), *Leuven Lecture notes,* Fifth year Master's program, 2001.

BLANCHARD, J. *Where was God On September 11?* Darlington, Massachusetts, 2002.

BLOESCH, D. G. *Crumbling Foundations. Death & Rebirth In An Age of Upheaval*, Michigan, 1984.

BOADT, L. & SMITH, M. S. (eds.), *Imagery and Imagination: Biblical Essays in Honor of Aloysius Fitzgerald, F. S. C.* (The Catholic Biblical Quarterly Monograph, Series 32), Washington, 2000.

BOFF, L. *Jesus Christ Liberator. A Critical Christology for Our Time,* New York, 1981.

BOFF, L. *Sacraments of Life. Life of the Sacraments. Story Theology.* D. John, (trans.), Beltsville MD, 1987.

BONHOEFFER, D. *Letters and Papers from Prison*, London, 1973.

BRAUMANN, R. *Afrika wird Totgefüttert. Plädoyer für eine neue Entwicklungspolitik,* Hamburg, Zurich, 1986.

BROWN, R. M. *Spirituality and Liberation*, Philadelphia, 1988.

BROTHER LAWRENCE, *The practice of the Presence of God*, Grand Rapids, 1967, Eighth Letter.

BRUEGGEMANN, W. *The Prophetic Imagination*, (second edition), New York, 2001.

CANDIDUS OF FULDA, "De Passione domini," 5; in J. P. MIGNE, *Patrologia Latina*, 106.68D-69A.

CARLYLE, T. *The French Revolution. A History*, Volume I (The Bastille), Volume II (The Constitution,), Volume III (The Guillotine) London, 1837, (Reprinted. 2001, The Folio Society, London).

CLAYBORNE, C. *The Autobiography of Martin Luther King, Jr.* New York, 2001.

CONGAR, Y. "The Role of the Church in the Modern World" in H. VORGRIMLER, (eds.), et al. *Commentary on the Documents of Vatican II* (Vol. V). *Pastoral Constitution on the Church in the Modern World,* New York, 1969.

CONGAR, Y. M-J. *Jalons pour une théologie du laïcat, Unam Sanctam 23,* Paris, 1953.

CROWDER, M., *The Story of Nigeria*, London, 1962.

CURTIS, M. (ed.) *Nature of Politics,* New York, 1962.

DANIEL-ROPS, H. *The Second Vatican Council. The Story*
Behind the Ecumenical Council of Pope John XIII, A. GUINAN
(Trans.) New York, 1962,

DE CHARDIN, P. T. *Le milieu divin essai de vie Intérieure,* Paris, 1957.

D'COSTA, G. *The Classic*, Cambridge, 1983.

D'COSTA, G. (ed.), *Christian Uniqueness Reconsidered: The Myth of a Pluralistic Theology of Religions,* New York, 1990.

DIE DEUTSCHEN BISCHÖFE, "Jesu Leben, sein Tod und seine Auferstehung als Anfang des wahren Friedens" in *Gerechter Friede*, no. 66, 27 September 2000, Bonn.

DOBSON, T. *How the Eucharist Can Transform Your Life*, New York, 1993.

GOLDBERG, M. *Theology and Narrative: A critical Introduction,* Nashville, 1982.

EASTERLY, W. *The White Man's Burden: Why the West's Efforts to Aid the Rest Have Done So Much Ill and So Little Good,* London, 2007.

EHUSANI, G. O. *An Afro-Christian Vision. "Ozovehe" Toward A More Humanized World,* Lanham, New York, 1991, (reprinted 1997, Ibadan.).

EHUSANI, G. O. *A Prophetic Church*, Ibadan, 1996.

EICHINGER, B. (ed.), *„50 Jahre Vatikanum II"*: Zentrale Veranstaltungen und Tipps für lokale Aktionen – vorbereitet und ausgearbeitet von der KEB in Bistum Regensburg e.V mit Ihren KooperationspartnerInnen, 10.Oktober 2011.

ELNOOD, D. J. (ed.), *Asian Christian Theology: Emerging Themes*, Philadelphia, 1980.

FARLEY, E. *Divine Empathy: A Theology of God*, Minneapolis, 1996.

FITZGERALD, A. D. O. S. A. (ed), *Augustine Through the Ages: An Encyclopedia,* Michigan, Cambridge, 1999.

GIBELLINI, J. R. (ed.), *Paths of African Theology*, New York,
1994.

GILES, J. A. (ed.), *Beati Lanfranci archiepiscopi Cantrarensis opera,* Vol. 2, Oxford, 1844.

GIRARD, R., *Le bouc émissaire*, Paris, 1982.

GOLDBERG, M. *Theology and Narrative: A critical Introduction,* Nashville, 1982.

GUTIERREZ, G. *Theology of Liberation*, London, 1978.

HAUERWAS, S. *After Christendom*, Nashville, 1991.

HAUERWAS, S. *The Peaceable Kingdom: A Primer in Christian Ethics,* Notre Dame, 1983.

HAUERWAS, S. *A Community of Character: Toward a Constructive Christian Social Ethic,* Notre Dame, 1981.

HAUERWAS, S. *Truthfulness and Tragedy: Further Investigations in Christian Ethics*, Notre Dame, 1977.

HAUERWAS, S. *After Christendom*, Nashville, 1991.

HAUERWAS, S. *Prayers Plainly Spoken*, Denver, 1999.

HICK, J. AND KNITTTER, P. (eds.), *The Myth of Christian Uniqueness: Toward a Pluralistic Theology of Religions,* New York, 1987.

HOWARD, J. W., *Corporatism and Comparative Politics*, New York, 1997.

HÜNERMANN U. P. & BERND JOCHEN HILBERATH, (Editors & co.), *Herders Theologischer Kommentar zum Zweiten Vatikanischen Konzil,* Band 5, Freiburg, Basel, Wien, 2009.

JOHN PAUL II, "Christifideles laici," in *Origins*. 18, 1989.

KATONGOLE, E. *Beyond Universal Reason. The Relation between Religion and Ethics in the Works of Stanley Hauerwas,* Notre Dame, 2000.

KENIS, L. *The Louvain Faculty of Theology in the Nineteenth Century. A Bibliography of the Professors in Theology and Canon Law, with Biographical Notes*, Leuven, 1994.

KINOTI, H.W, & WALIGGO, J.M (eds.), *The Bible in African Christianity: Essays in Biblical Theology*, Nairobi, 1997.

KOELBER, J. F. *Vatican II and Phenomenology. Reflections on the Life-World of the Church*, Boston, 1985.

KORNPROBST, R. (Hg.), *Freude ist Gebet: Worte von Mutter Teresa*, Kevelaer, 2010.

KUKAH, M. H. *Democracy and Civil Society in Nigeria*, Ibadan, 1999.

KÜNG, H. (ed.), *Yes To A Global Ethic*, London, 1996.

KÜNG, H. "Global Politics and Global Ethic," *Unpublished Lecture*, Brussels, March 9, 2000.

LAKELAND, P. *Post Modernity. Christian Identity In A fragmented Age. Guides to Theological Inquiry*, Minneapolis, 1997.

LAMBERTS, J. (ed.), *Hedendaagse Accenten in de Sacramentologie*, Leuven, 1994.

LONGENECKER. R. N. (edited), *The Road from Damascus. The Impact of Paul's Conversion on His life, Thought, and Ministry*, Michigan, Cambridge, 1997.

MacHAFFIE, B. J. *Her Story. Women In Christian Tradition*, Philadelphia, 1986.

MacINTYRE, A. *Whose Justice? Which Rationality*? Notre Dame, 1988.

MacINTYRE, A. *After Virtue. A Study in Moral Theory,* (second edition), London, 1997.

Maloney, G. A. *Mysticism and The new Age; Christic Consciousness in the new Creation,* New York, 1991.

McAFEE BROWN, R. *Spirituality and liberation. Overcoming the Great fallacy*, London, 1988.

MERRIGAN, T. & HAERS, J. (eds.), *The Myriad Christ. Plurality and the Quest for Unity in Contemporary Christology*, Leuven, 2000.

MERTZ, T. (Hg), *Mit dem Heiligen Vater durch das Jahr: Ein Lesebuch*, Augsburg, 2008, s. 135/6.

MEYER, J., *Beauty for Ashes. Receiving Emotional Healing*, New York, 2003.

MIGNE, J. P. *Patrologia Latina*, 106.68D-69A.

MILBANK, J. *Theology and Social Theory*, Cambridge, 1991.

MOLTMANN, J. *Experiences in Theology. Ways and Forms of Christian Theology,* M. KOHL (trans.), Minneapolis, 2000.

MOYO, D. *Dead Aid: Why Aid Is Not Working and How There Is a Better Way for Africa*, Farrar, Straus and Giroux, 2009.

MUDGE, L. S., "Hermeneutics" in A. Richardson & J. BOWDEN (eds.), *The Westminster Dictionary of Christian Theology,* Philadelphia, 1983.

MUELLER-VOLLMER, K. (ed.), *The Hermeneutics Reader,* New York, 1990.

MUELLER D. L. *Foundation of Karl Barth's Doctrine of Reconciliation, Jesus Christ Crucified and Risen* (Toronto Studies in Theology, 54), 1991.

NEIRYNCK, F. *De theologische faculteit 1919–1969* (Leuven, 1970)

NEWBIGIN, L. *Truth and Authority in Modernity.* (In the series, "Christian Mission and Modern Culture"), Pennsylvania, 1996.

NICOLAS, M-J. *Théologie de la resurrection. Jesus la resurrection et la vie,* Toulouse, 1982.

NUSSBAUM, M. *The Fragility of Goodness*, New York, 1986.

OKERE, T. *African Philosophy. A Historico-Hermeneutical Investigation of the Conditions of its Possibility,* New York, 1983.

OKUMA, P. C. *Understanding Human Work and Dignity*, Enugu, 1997.

OKUMA, P. C. *A Call to Authentic Living in Christ: The Challenge of the Third Millennium,* Enugu, 1998.

OKUMA, P. C. *Towards an African Theology. The Igbo Context in Nigeria,* Brussels, 2002.

OZIGBOH, R. A. *Igbo Catholicism: The Onitsha Connection 1967–1984,* Onitsha, 1985.

PHILIPS, G. *The Role of the Laity in the Church*, GILBERT, J. R. & MOUDRY, J. W. (trans.), Cork, 1955.

Parliament of the World's Religion in *Declaration toward a Global Ethic* Chicago, U.S.A, 4 September 1993.

Politeia Conference, *Political Communication: The Rise of Lifestyle Politics and Its Consequences for Liberty*, Brussels, May 3rd, 2002.

POWER, D. N. *Sacrament: The Language of God's Giving,* New York, 1999.

Publik-Forum, Zeitung Kritischer Christen, 25 January 2002.

Publik-Forum. Zeitung Kritischer Christen, no.4, 22 February 2002.

RAHNER, K. *Theological Investigations. Man in the Church.* Vol. II, K. H. Kruger (transl.), Baltimore, London, 1963.

RAHNER, K. "Considerations on the Active Role of the Person in the Sacramental Event," in *Theological Investigations*, Vol.14, Baltimore, Helicon, New York 1976.

RAHNER, K. et al. (eds.), *Sacramantum Mundi. An Enclopaedia of Theology,* Vol. 2, Basle- Montreal, 1978.

RATZINGER, J. KARDINAL, *Salz der Erde. Ein Gesprach mit Peter Seewald,* Stuttgart, 1998.

RATZINGER, J. POPE BENEDICT XVI, *Jesus of Nazareth – Holy Week: From the Entrance into the Jerusalem to the Resurrection,* San Francisco, 2011.

SACHS, J. *The End of Poverty. How we can make it happen in our Lifetime*, London, 2005.

SCOLOZZI, ANGELO. D (ed.), MOTHER TERESA, *Thirsting for God: A yearbook of prayers, Meditations, and Anecdotes,* Cincinnati, 2000.

RAHNER, K. *Theological Investigations. Man in the Church.* Vol. II, K. H. Kruger (transl.), Baltimore, London, 1963.

REICH, R. *L'économie mondialisée*, Paris, 1993, p.103, quoted in F. Houtart, *The World-Encompassment of the Economy*, in CQ 68(1993–94) 2–10.

RICHARD, L. O. M. I, et. al. (eds.), *Vatican II. The Unfinished Agenda. A look to the Future,* New York, 1987.

RICOEUR, P. *Freud and Philosophy. An Essay on Interpretation,* Connecticut, 1970.

RICOEUR, P. *Hermeneutics and the human sciences*, trans and edited by THOMPSON, J. B. New York, 1980.

RICOEUR, P. *Soi-même comme un autre (l'ordre philosophique),* Paris 1990.

RICOEUR, P. *Time and Narrative* (3 Volumes), MCLAUGHLIN, K. & PELLAUER, D. (translated), Chicago, 1984–1988.

SCHERER, J. A. & BEVANS, S. B. (eds.) Vol. 2, New York, 1994. *New Directions in Mission & Evangelization. Theological Foundations*, New York, 1994.

SCHILLEBEECKX, E. *Christ: The Experience of Jesus As Lord,* BOWDEN, J. (translated), New York, 1989.

SCHINELLER, P. *A Handbook on Inculturation*, New York, 1990.

SCHWÖBEL, C. (Conference paper), *God as Conversation. Reflections on a Theological Ontology of Communicative Relations,* Leuven, November 7, 2001.

SCOLOZZI, A. D. (Complier), *Mother Teresa: Thirsting for God – A Yearbook of prayers, Meditations and Anecdotes*, Cincinnati, 2000.

SHEEN, F. J. *Christ-centered Wisdom for the Third Millennium*, Missouri, 1999.

SHEEN, F. J., *Wits and Wisdom*, New York, 1969.

SMITH, S. G. "Three Religious Attitudes" in P. ROSSI, (eds.), *Philosophy and Theology*, Marquette University Journal, Vol.11, No.1, 3.

SOBRINO, J. *The Principle of Mercy: Taking the Crucified People from the Cross,* New York, 1984.

STACPOLE, A. (ed), *Vatican II by Those Who Were There*, London, 1986.

STEXHE DE & VERSTRATEN J. *Matters of Breath: Foundations for Professional Ethics (European Ethics Network Core Materials for the Development of Courses in Professional Ethics),* Leuven, 2000.

TANNER, N. P. S. J. (ed.) *Decrees of the Ecumenical Councils, Vol. II (Trent to Vatican II),* London, 1990.

THE CATECHISM OF THE CATHOLIC CHURCH, English translation, Kenya, 1995.

The New Jerusalem Bible (Standard Edition) London, 1985.

THE CATHOLIC BISHOPS' CONFERENCE OF NIGERIA, *The Eucharist and Unity.* 1992, nr. 27.

THOMASSET, A. *Poétique de l'existence et agir moral en société. La contribution de Paul Ricoeur au fondement d'une éthique herméneutique et narrative, dans une perspective chrétienne,* Louvain, 1995.

TILLICH, P. *Dynamics of Faith*, New York, 1957.

World Council of Churches, *Towards an Ethic of Global Responsibility,* Chicago, U.S.A. 4 September 1993.

Urs von BALTHASAR, H. *Mysterium Paschale: The Mystery of Easter*, NICHOLS, A. (translated), Michigan, 1990.

VERSTRAETEN, J. "The 'World' of the Bible as Meta-Ethical Framework of Meaning for Ethics: An Interpretation," in VROOM, H. M. & GORT, J. D., (eds.), Holy *Scriptures in Judaism, Christianity and Islam. Hermeneutics, Values and Society,* Amsterdam/Atlanta, 1997.

VERSTRAETEN, J. (trans.), *The Rediscovery of Meaning in Professional life: Perspectives for Spirituality of the Laity in the Twenty-first Century,* Leuven, 1999.

VERSTRAETEN, J, *Beyond Business Ethics: Leadership, Spirituality and the Quest for Meaning,* Leuven, 2000.

WEBER, M. *Essays in Sociology,* Oxford, New York, 1946.

WARREN, R. *The Purpose Driven Life; What on Earth am I Here for*? Michigan, 2002.

WITTGENSTEIN, L. *Philosophical Investigations.* ANSCOMBE, E. (trans.), New York, 1953.

WYSZINKI, S. *All You Who Labour: Work and the Sanctification of daily life,* Manchester, 1995.

B. JOURNALS, NEWSPAPERS, MAGAZINES AND DICTIONARIES

Philosophy and Theology. Marquette University Journal, Vol.11, no. 1(1998).

The Pope Speaks, Vol. 47, no.3.

Encounter. A Journal of African Life and Religion, Vol. 3, Rome, 1994.
Theological Studies, 55 (1994), 661.

L'Osservatore Romano, (English edition), February 26, 1979.

L'OSSERVATORE ROMANO, February 26, 1979.

THE ECONOMIST MAGAZINE, 11 April 1998

TIME MAGAZINE, May 29, 2000.

THE ECONOMIST, August 7, 1999.

THE FORTUNE MAGAZINE, March 13, 2000.

THE ECONOMIST, AUGUST 7, 1999.

THE COMMONWEAL: A review of Religion, Politics and Culture, September 22, 2000.

TIME MAGAZINE, April 13, 1998.

WEBSTER'S POCKET BUSINESS DICTIONARY (New Revised Edition), 1997.

C. WEBSITES

- Http://www.eisf.eu/resources/library/hum_action_mil_privatisation.pdf, consulted on 05/09/2012.
- CatholicCulture.org: http://www.catholicculture.org/culture/library/view.cfm?recnum=5643, consulted on 22 November 2012.
- Http://www.vatican.va/archive/ccc_css/archive/catechism/p2s2c1a1.htm consulted on 22.11.2012.
- Http://www.guardian.co.uk/global-development/2012/apr/17/nigeria-governor-james-ibori-sentenced, consulted on May 19, 2012.
- *Http://www.shortnews.de/id/971025/* – 30/10/2012.
- Http://dictionary.reference.com/browse/theandric consulted on 30/10/2012

Appendix

Other Books by Peter Chidi Okuma published by Peter Lang Academic Publishers:

1. Towards an African Theology. The Igbo Context in Nigeria, Peter Lang Publishers, Bruxelles, Frankfurt, Bern, New York, Oxford, 2002.
2. OMUMU – THE IGBO LIFE-VALUE: A CHALLENGE TO HUMAN LIFE ISSUE TODAY (with Particular Focus on *Humanae Vitae* In light of Familial value study) – An Analytical-Practical Approach, Peter Lang Publishers, Frankfurt am Main, New York, 2008.
3. EMPOWERMENT OF THE CATHOLIC LAITY IN THE NIGERIAN POLITICAL SITUATION. A Hermeneutical Reading of *Apostolicam Actuositatem* (the decree on the Apostolate of the Laity of Vatican II and it's application to concrete situation, Peter Lang Academic Publishers, Frankfurt am Main, New York, 2008.
4. THE VATICAN II: THE LAITY AND TODAY'S CHALLENGES, Peter Lang Academic Publishers, Frankfurt am Main, New York, 2011.